# Chiropractor:
## The Quest for Professional Respect

## Kent L. Boyer

Austin & Winfield
San Francisco, 1993

# Chiropractor:
## The Quest for
## Professional Respect

## Kent L. Boyer

Austin & Winfield
San Francisco, 1993

*Library of Congress Cataloging-in-Publication Data*


Boyer, Kent L.
   Chiropractor : the quest for professional respect / Kent L. Boyer.
      p.   cm.
   ISBN 1-880921-47-2 : $29.95
   1. Chiropractic--Vocational guidance.  2. Chiropractors.
3. Chiropractic--public opinion.  4. Chiropractors--Public opinion.
I. Title.
RZ236.B693  1993
615.5'34--dc20                                     93-28885
                                                   CIP





Austin & Winfield, Publishers
P.O.Box 2529
San Francisco, CA  94133

# **<u>Dedication</u>**

To Guy and Joan Boyer, two of my favorite people.

# **<u>Preface</u>**

In my previous book, *How to Succeed in Chiropractic College*, I explored the experience of going to college to become a Doctor of Chiropractic (DC). That book ended appropriately on graduation day with all the hopes and dreams that a new beginning brings. This book is about events in the life of a practicing chiropractor, events shaped by public perception, media, and the existing hierarchy of the health care system.

Writing this book has required me to carefully straddle a rather tall fence. Because I am a chiropractor and a chiropractic college administrator, I am perhaps overly sensitive about criticizing my own profession in public. On the other hand, I am aware that criticism of the traditional health system by a chiropractor may sound like sour grapes. I am somewhat concerned that someone or some group may be offended by something I write. I am aware that students whose paths have or will cross with mine will be reading this book. As sensitive as I am to these delicate issues, I still want to write my observations about practicing chiropractic health care.

I think I have arrived at a fair solution for the above concerns. I have decided just to be honest about what it was like *for me* to practice as a chiropractor in Iowa in the late 1980s. I would not presume to generalize that all chiropractors have had similar experiences or feelings. This is the way it happened for me.

I have always been suspicious of health claims made without scientific substantiation. I was cautious of these types of claims even while I was in chiropractic college. I think that this skepticism has given me an unusual outlook on chiropractic since anecdotal or empirical evidence has been the cornerstone of the chiropractic explanation for decades. Only in the past few years has research been done to begin to answer questions about chiropractic therapy. As my students know, I am a firm proponent for the continued need for research in the chiropractic profession.

Having said that, I must tell you that many of the positive results I had with patients as a practicing chiropractor have no conclusive explanation in the scientific literature. I offer these stories as a part of my experience. I have not attempted to explain why they occurred, nor have I edited them to make them sound either good or bad for chiropractic. I have not offered them in any way as a form of self-aggrandizement. These experiences happened, so I am telling you about them. Explanation of the hows and whys will come in the research of the years to come.

If you are about to read this book because you think it is a book about how chiropractic is the greatest health profession known to man or if you hope that this is a book bashing the medical profession, you are about to be disappointed. While I obviously feel that chiropractic is a worthwhile and important health service, I have never felt that disrespect for, or maligning of other professions does anything to elevate chiropractic. On the other hand, if you thought this was a book warning the public against chiropractic, take the book back. But if you are interested in learning about what it is like to practice as a chiropractor in a traditionally medically oriented society, I think you will find what I have written to be very interesting indeed.

I have several target audiences in mind as I begin to write this book. I am writing for chiropractic students and those who are considering chiropractic as a career. They are more interested in "what's it really like" stories than embellished career book or college catalog descriptions. I am also writing this book with the hope that other medical professionals will find it informative, as I have been fascinated by practices described in print by veterinarian James Herriott, psychiatrist David Viscott, midwife Penny Armstrong, and surgeon William Nolen. Also I think medical sociology students, who usually learn very little about non-traditional health professions, should hear about chiropractic from a chiropractor. Finally, there are a lot of interested and informed health consumers who have an interest in books about health professions.

Across the face of health care, the roles of the players are being challenged and expanded. The medical doctor is no longer seen, by patients or other providers, as the ultimate end-all voice in health care. Chiropractic has been viewed as a challenger of the medical profession for almost one hundred years now. Chiropractors used to want to maintain an isolation from other health professionals, but recently have begun to position themselves for a larger and more integrated role in mainstream health care. Nurses, pharmacists, and physical therapists have also begun to challenge the medical system for more autonomous roles in patient care. The old, honored medical hierarchy is changing.

Do chiropractors, nurses, and others and suffer from a sort of professional low self esteem because they are not medical doctors? Are these professions on a quest for respect within the system? Do the behaviors of these professions suggest that they feel they are second-class citizens even as they challenge the medical hierarchy? Do these feelings and behaviors affect patient access, referral patterns and decision making? If they do, how does this affect patient care?  Can reform of this system, with the patient's best interest in mind, actually occur?

In all segments of society, reformation of a time-honored system comes slowly and seldom smoothly.  We are in the midst of such a revolution in health care today.  Some would argue that the reformation of the health system is due entirely to economics, a topic which I have chosen not to discuss in great detail in this work.  While I agree that economics are, to a large degree, changing the tenor of the system, I wish to concentrate instead on the sociological roots of change.  Dissatisfaction with the system and the roles that various providers played in the system are at least as important to the story as the economics of it.  The story of the reformation of the health system is a story of people and the response of the patients they serve.  In that light, this book attempts to tell the story of the chiropractor's quest for professional respect in a changing professional world.

Kent L. Boyer, D.C.
Dallas, Texas
May, 1993

# Table of Contents

# 1

# <u>Graduation and Beyond</u>

Why do people choose to become doctors?  What is it about a health care career that appeals to people?  What do these careers offer people which make them attractive?

Usually the first on the list is the issue of respect.  Even in todays climate of jaded skepticism toward doctors, there is a certain respect afforded to people who have chosen to make health care their career.  Why?

The public is generally aware of the educational commitment that a doctor has made to ultimately earn his or her degree.  Far less people realize that a doctor of chiropractic has made a similar, although admittedly, a slightly shorter commitment.  This commitment alone deserves, I think, a modicum of respect.  This book will help to explain the educational commitment a chiropractor must make.  The fact that many people don't understand the depth of the commitment for the chiropractic doctor is one of the reasons that the controversy over chiropractic continues.

Respect is also afforded due to the nature of the service which various types of doctors perform in our society.  For example, emergency room doctors are, rightly, I think, afforded respect for the nature of the work that they perform.  Often, a patient has been in a car accident or has had a heart attack, and would die without the timely ministrations of this person.  Clearly, the emergency room doctor deserves the respect and gratitude of the patient who may live or die based on his/her call. What, then, about health care professionals who don't routinely deal with life and death health issues? Do they deserve the same kind of gratitude and respect?

* * *

Joe, age 35, and his family had been patients previously. I had treated Joe for low back and leg pain which was aggravated by his career as a mechanic. I was currently seeing him on a health maintenance schedule when his wife called early one morning.

"Joe is on his way into town," she said. "Can you work him in this morning?" She sounded agitated.

When I came into the treatment room, Joe was sitting on the edge of the table with his shirt off. He didn't wait for me to close the door before he began talking.

"Doc, I thought I was having a heart attack last night. I had chest pains and I couldn't take a deep breath without excruciating pain. Peggy called our medical doctor and he sent me to the hospital emergency room for an EKG, but it was normal. They said it was probably just something I ate, and that it would go away. I couldn't get any sleep last night, and I know something is wrong."

He looked at me, the story completed. It was my turn.

As it turned out, Joe had an acute rib joint dysfunction which caused pain on every breath and sent pain around his rib cage to the front of his body. The problem was rather easily corrected by restoring motion to the affected joints. Not knowing what the problem was, he had been right to follow through with the EKG. However, it wasn't his cardiovascular system which was affected at all. Rather, it was his musculoskeletal system. Even though the pain was acute, the situation wasn't a life or death one. At least he ended up in the right office as his second choice.

Should the chiropractor, who diagnoses and successfully treats a musculoskeletal problem like Joe's be afforded the same amount of respect as the emergency room doctor?

* * *

Chiropractic doctors more often deal with patients with chronic ailments which have robbed them of a certain quality of life. The restoration of that quality of life is very important to the patients of the chiropractor. It's not emergency heart surgery, but the ability for a young mother to be able to pick her small children up without pain; the father to be able to return to his physically demanding job to support his family; the ability of the elderly lady to return to doing needlepoint or knitting when pain or disability had prevented that is often a welcome quality of life improvement.

Chiropractic medicine suffers from a misconception in certain sectors of society that it is not a necessary health service because it doesn't deal with life and death emergency health care. In my classes with beginning students, I often compare the public attitude toward chiropractic to cosmetic surgery. No one would suggest that persons who have suffered accidental disfigurement should be denied the services of a cosmetic surgeon to help restore them to a degree of normalcy. But our society would be hard pressed to authorize federal payment for a face lift or "nose job" for a welfare mother. When chiropractic is perceived to be nothing more than a "feel-good" type of health service, it is perhaps understandable why the profession suffers from a lack of respect in the health community. Education about the profession will show that chiropractic has more to offer society than a temporary good feeling.

It is my opinion that a career choice which considers respect for oneself and one's profession important is justifiable and desirable. I think that a doctor of chiropractic is deserving of that respect.

All persons in a capitalist society must consider financial reward when they make career choices. We all work for compensation, and people who choose careers in health care are no exception. The interesting irony about health care is that patients don't want to pay for it. Businessmen understand the need for profit in their businesses, but make that businessman a patient and he doesn't want his health care providers to profit. Witness the current attitiude of the population that someone else should be responsible for paying their health care bills. It should be the insurance company's problem, or their employer, or the federal government, but certainly not an individual responsibility. This thinking sometimes produces an unwarranted suspicion about the motives of health care providers.

To tell health care providers that they are selfish for wanting to be paid for the professional service they provide is hypocritical at best. To suggest to people who are choosing health care careers that they should make that choice without considering financial reward is unrealistic. Many, then, choose all types of health care for prospective financial rewards. However, if this consideration is the only one, the prospective provider has probably missed the secret of most providers' success. I think that this secret is that health care providers who are happy with their career choice have a strong altruistic sense in addition to wanting to be compensated for their efforts.

Health care is a service profession in much the same way that retail sales or customer service careers are. Health care deals with a different basic need, but it is still a career which recognizes and meets certain needs of the public.  Anyone who has worked with the public, whether at a McDonalds or at a department store will tell you that dealing with the public can, at times, be difficult.  Health care is no different.

* * *

I was preparing for a busy Saturday morning in my office when the telephone rang.  My receptionist had not yet arrived, so I picked up the phone.  On the other end was a woman who explained that she couldn't get a hold of her regular chiropractor that morning.  She had to make a three hour drive due to an illness in the family, and her low back was bothering her. She didn't think that she could make the drive without some relief.

I have always been an easy target for human suffering.  Even though my Saturday morning was booked solid, I agreed to take a look at her if she came right over.

I did as thorough an assessment as I could without having access to her previous records.  She had a history of chronic low back pain which had always responded to chiropractic manipulation.  I explained to her that there were certain types of adjustments that I could not perform without more information, but that I felt I could improve her joint function and at least help her through the weekend.  I proceeded to treat her.

After the adjustment, she told me that her regular chiropractor usually treated her with ultrasound therapy in addition to manipulation.  I felt that ultrasound may provide some temporary relief, and proceeded to administer the treatment.

When we got to the waiting room, my receptionist had still not yet arrived.  I decided to charge her only for the adjustment and ultrasound, even though I would have been justified in adding a brief exam charge as well as a charge for seeing her before regular hours.  I felt for her, however, and had been glad I could help.

When I told her what the charge was, she bristled.  "You mean you're charging me extra for the ultrasound?  My regular chiropractor just has one office charge no matter what he does," she exclaimed indignantly.

I overcame my surprise and anger to explain that in my office, the fee was based on what services were provided.  I didn't add that I could easily charge extra for doing her the favor of seeing her at 7:30 in the morning.

"I'llnever come back here again," she spat as she wrote the check and stormed out.  Some patients have no gratitude for the services of a health professional.

* * *

Persons who are considering a career in the health care field, then, should have the type of personality which finds that serving people is a worthwhile activity.  They should find pleasure in meeting people during a time of need and helping them with their specialized knowledge and service.

Potential health care providers who want respect and financial reward but don't have this strong service attitude are a danger to the public.  Many of these providers work essentially alone and the possibility of unethical behavior for personal reward is great.

I have interviewed many candidates for admission into chiropractic colleges.  When I interview these men and women, I try to find out why the candidate wants to be a doctor of chiropractic, and if he or she has considered both the benefits and the costs of the career appropriately.  Most of the potential students are afraid to say that they want to make a good living, or that they desire to respect themselves and  have the respect of the patients they serve. Most interviewees think that the only reason I want to hear is that they want to help people.

In reality, persons who choose chiropractic for all of the above reasons will probably not be disappointed in their career choice. This is especially true if they have a realistic view of the state of the health care system and chiropractic's role within that system.

* * *

Why would a person choose chiropractic as a profession rather than medicine or dentistry?

I think that many young people feel that there is little difference in respect, satisfaction, or earning power between the professions. Dentists, medical doctors, podiatrists, and chiropractors are all doctors, they reason, so the rewards of the professions must be about the same.

I hope to show you that chiropractic, like any of the health professions, cannot and should not be compared to other health professions. Each of these professions has its own peculiarities. They are not the same.

Many of the students found in a chiropractic institution used to be grateful patients or relatives of a chiropractor. We do understand that if a person has had a particularly successful experience as a chiropractic patient, he/she might consider chiropractic as a career. We also understand that in certain families, it is common for sons and daughters to follow in the career footsteps of a successful or happy parent or other relative.

One interesting phenomena that chiropractic educators are noticing lately is the rising number of entering chiropractic students who have never visited a chiropractor or know one personally. There is a new group of chiropractic students today who have chosen chiropractic health care for a completely different reason.

Some are students who have been interested in a medical career of some type and have investigated many health careers. They have decided for a variety of reasons that chiropractic is the career for them.

The past couple of decades have seen an enormous increase in interest in natural healing, health, and wellness. Chiropractic health care is perceived as a natural healing method because of its non-pharmacological, non-surgical approach to health. Some choices for a career in chiropractic come from an interest in this natural approach.

Chiropractic is also seen as a conservative health approach, free from the excesses of modern medicine which has been under so much fire in the media and society of late. Some students choose chiropractic because they perceive that it is much less invasive, free from potential side effects of drugs and surgery, and a "cleaner" health profession. Some of this philosophy I can attest is true, some is a misperception of the field.

There has been an explosion of interest from the athletic world in chiropractic health care in the recent past. Chiropractors treat professional athletes, olympic teams as well as weekend athletes with some regularity. Many prospective students get into chiropractic because of this athletic interest.

Unfortunately for the profession of chiropractic, there is a lingering misconception that chiropractic health care has mystical or religious overtones which appeals to a certain group of prospective students. Modern chiropractic science is neither a religion or a mystical practice; rather, it is based on clinical science and research. These students are disappointed in their career choice and some do not finish chiropractic college. If they do finish college,

I am afraid that they continue to cast aspersions on the profession by promoting chiropractic as a sort of new age religion.

And then we have the second career prospective chiropractors. Let's divide them into two groups: those who have had a career in health as another type of professional, and those who have had a previous career outside of health.

I have had the pleasure of teaching many nurses, physical therapists, pharmacists, emergency technicians and an occasional medical doctor to be chiropractors. Most of these students, as would be expected, are excellent, dedicated students. I have always been interested in why they left their first profession and why they chose chiropractic as their second profession. While the reasons are as varied as the students themselves, many of them talk about a dissatisfaction with their first career that was so great, they chose to leave it and start a second career.

Nurses and physical therapists often talk about a lack of autonomy in their first professions which became harder and harder to deal with as they interacted with patients. While both professions offer further education which would lead to more autonomy as a nurse or physical therapist, many of these second career chiropractic students also have become disillusioned with the traditional medical system of which they were a part.

For pharmacists, the complaint is often that their education is not being used in functioning primarily as a prescription-filler in a drug store or hospital. Many of these students want more contact with the patient than they have as a pharmacist. A number of these students are also particularly interested in chiropractic because of the non-pharmacological approach to health. This approach presumably appeals to some pharmacists because of their experience with what they consider excesses in the pharmacological approach to health care.

* * *

Many second career chiropractic students have not been involved in health care in their previous careers, or, like me, were nominally involved as a para-professional.  I had worked as a hospital orderly in my early twenties, but had left that job in search of a career and to earn more money.  After a successful albeit short career in retail management, I decided that returning to college to earn a degree would be worth the price.  I never really considered anything but health care, although I wasn't sure what kind of a health care provider I wanted to be.

I didn't seriously consider medical school for three reasons.  First, I had heard the rumors of the competition for a seat in medical school, and the necessity of a 4.0 grade point average.  I had been an A and B student in my two years of college, but I had nowhere near a four point.  I had never allowed myself to get too stressed out about grades, probably because I was originally an art major, a major which is not well known for its academic difficulty.  I didn't think I had the grades for medical school, and grades weren't supremely important to me.

Second, I thought that at twenty-eight, I was probably beyond the age of students that medical schools typically admitted.  I would have had to complete a bachelor's degree before medical school, which would have made me thirty by the time I entered medical school.  Assuming that I could have gotten into a medical school, I would have been thirty-four before I graduated.  Then, depending on the specialty that I entered, my residency would have been three or more years.  I did understand the concept of delayed gratification, but I was already married eight years at the time, and had a seven year old child.  I felt that I was simply too old.

Because I already lived in a city that had a chiropractic college, this choice was the easiest one for me and my family. Chiropractic didn't require a bachelor's degree; in fact, I already had enough undergraduate hours to enter chiropractic college, but they weren't in the right subject matter. I would have to go back to college, but only for a year or so before I could get into chiropractic college. The chiropractic program could be completed taking no summers off, thus completing a four academic year program in three calendar years.

I had been a chiropractic patient once as a kid and more recently with a rather severe episode of low back pain. I didn't know much about the science of chiropractic, but I knew that I had gotten good results with chiropractic care and that many other people had, too. The decision was made.

I would suspect that many second career people make their decision to enter chiropractic college for some of the same reasons that I did. Some do not have any health care experience, but have always been interested in health care. At a certain time in their first careers, it becomes possible for them to look into making this change.

* * *

My graduation day, June 12, 1987, arrived approximately four years after I had made the decision to return to college. My first task had been to complete thirty-four semester hours of college work in less than one year. For financial reasons, I continued to work full time at my retail management job with JCPenney for the first semester while I took Biology and Inorganic Chemistry at a near-by community college. I would leave for work at 7:30 in the morning, and get home twelve to fourteen hours later, Monday through

Thursday.  I had not studied biology since my sophomore year in high school some twelve years before, and I had never taken chemistry.  The schedule was extraordinarily difficult.  So difficult that by November, I was working out a plan which would allow me to quit my job after Christmas and attend college full time in the spring semester.

This accomplished, I enrolled in twenty-six semester hours of work at two separate colleges - History, Psychology, Anatomy and Physiology, and Inorganic Chemistry at the community college, and Organic Chemistry and Physics at another college.  I was still gone from home morning through evening.  As harried as I was, I don't remember ever considering quitting or slowing down.

What I do remember about those months was rediscovering that I loved learning and going to school.  I recall writing in a birthday card to my wife my thanks for her support for this hair-brained scheme of mine.  I ended up with As and Bs in all these courses (a good years worth of education in five months), and a seat in the July, 1984 entering class at Palmer College of Chiropractic.

By the time I was ready to graduate, I was just excited to be done.  I had worked hard for thirty-six straight months and I was stressed out, tired of playing games and jumping through hoops.  While I didn't expect my graduation day to be anything special, it turned out to be just that in spite of my expectations.  I have written before that there was a closing of that chapter of my life which I felt on graduation day.

I didn't invite any guests except my wife, son and my dad, who had taken the day off from his assembly line job at John Deere.  My wife had invited her new friend, the wife of a neighbor who was getting ready to start Palmer.

As the processional began and we started to march into the auditorium, I began to feel proud that I had actually completed the maze. I knew my wife was proud of me, and my dad, but I still wasn't sure that I was proud to be graduating as a chiropractor. I was worried still about the controversies within and outside the profession.

I had gone through school skeptical at every turn, determined not to swallow anything that was taught to me unless I could back it up in journals or books. Many of my classmates weren't so hard to convince. This unfortunate habit ended up costing me thousands of dollars in books, and hundreds of hours in the library copying research papers. At least I knew what I knew, and I think it could safely be said that for the most part, I graduated in spite of my teachers rather than because of them. I didn't fully appreciate many of my teachers until years later.

The graduation was over and all the proud families were taking pictures. My friend Greg's girlfriend aimed my new 35 mm camera (a graduation present from my wife) at my wife and I, and other pictures were taken with Greg and my other buddy, Joe. In all the excitement, I forgot to have my picture taken with my dad, a faux pas which still hurts me when I think about it today.

My dad has one of the strongest work ethics of anyone that I know. For my entire life, he worked at factories in the Quad Cities, then known as the farm implement capitol of the world. I have early memories of my parents telling my brother and I that they didn't want us to ever work in a factory, that we should go to college and aim for something higher. I don't know when the thought first struck me that I knew my dad was unhappy with his work. Though I knew he didn't want me to end up working at John Deere, I never heard him complain about going to work and I bet I could count on two hands the number of days that he missed work during my entire childhood.

I think now that Mom and Dad's insistence that my brother and I not work in a factory must have had a great effect on all of my career plans. I have always valued careers which allow you to earn money with your brains and not muscles. This undoubtedly came from watching my dad work hard at a hot in the summer, cold in the winter assembly line job. I remember the small shavings of metal that somehow got into his hands even though he wore gloves, the special soap that he used to clean the grime from his hands, and how they cracked and bled in the winter. This made a powerful impression on me.

So, when I went off to college as an 18 year old, dad was proud. When I worked in a bank, dad was proud. When I worked as a hospital orderly, dad was proud. When I sold real estate, dad was proud. When I was successful for five years as a retail manger, dad was proud. Then he was proud that I was a chiropractic student. It must have made him extraordinarily proud to see me graduate.

I think my wife felt very proud, too, but she also felt, I think, a great sense of relief that it was all over. Financial worries had begun to consume both of us - me first because I tried to hide from her how deeply in debt we were as a result of my education, but then she began to feel the gnawing worry, too. But after that graduation day, I would be earning money again. We hoped  and prayed.

I witnessed my classmates and friends sharing their pride with their families... I saw the pride in my family's faces, but inside I wasn't sure how proud I was. I was concerned about how much respect I would be shown, how much money I would make, and whether or not my career would be challenging. Would the health care system accept me as a DC? What was in the future for the chiropractic profession?

It is common and, I think appropriate for chiropractic students to wonder about these things. Thoughtful consideration over such issues makes for eventual solutions and strategies which can't help but strengthen the profession.


* * *


Becoming a doctor of chiropractic resulted in costs for me as well as benefits.

What had my education cost me? There was a definite cost to my family life. I am expert now at counseling students about how to keep their marriage going during school, and maybe I'm so good at that advice because mine almost ended during this time. "Whatever I did, do the opposite and it will work out," should be my advice. I had been married eight years when I started back to school. I had a son who was seven years old. We had been the stereotypical nuclear family - doing everything together, spending every leisure moment together. All of a sudden, after I started school, all of this changed. Our lives became my wife and son in one corner, and myself alone in another. I was such an obsessive student that I just didn't have much time for them anymore. Even when I wasn't studying, I'm afraid that I wasn't much fun to be with.

I tried much harder with my son than I did with my wife. I picked him up from school every day and spent the late afternoon with him. These were precious times for me as I questioned him about school and he glibly talked to me about everything that had gone on. During this period we started the habit of asking each other what we had for lunch. I still ask him, but high school kids don't talk about such inane things, so sometimes he won't tell me now.

I was in chiropractic school during my son's second through fourth grades. He went to a Lutheran school, and almost every night he had homework. Not because he wasn't doing well (he has always been an excellent student), but because the school had high expectations for the kids. So we would go home, work on his homework, maybe watch *Gumby* or *Leave It To Beaver* on TV, and then make supper together and wait for mom to get home. After supper, I retreated to my bedroom/office to study until 9:00. Every night. For thirty-six months. On Saturday, I would get up late (about 9:00), get dressed, and study until about 4:00 or so. On Sunday, I would do my washing and ironing for the week in the morning and study in the afternoon. Monday, I was up at 5:00 a.m. again, starting the whole process over. The commitment was much greater than I had anticipated.

Chiropractic education is expensive. Since all of the accredited chiropractic colleges in the country are free standing educational institutions, tuition is quite high. Relationships with state university systems would presumably not only lower tuition, but would have other benefits as well. The school I entered charged about fifteen hundred dollars per term. At twelve terms, the figure for tuition alone was about eighteen thousand dollars. This figure has now ballooned so that the student can expect tuition for the program to cost about forty thousand dollars. Books and supplies (which are extraordinarily expensive in any medical field) can easily top five thousand dollars, so that forty-five thousand dollars just to complete the program is not unusual. Many students enter chiropractic college with debts from undergraduate school, too, so that figure must be added into the equation. I have taught many students who work part-time during the educational experience, but for me the small amount of money that I could have made would have just been spent getting a babysitter for my son. In addition, I was so stressed out during the initial years of the program, that I don't think I could have dealt with the additional stress of going to a job every day. Most of us who are in chiropractic education discourage students who want to work, at least in the first two academic years of the program. Therefore, most students must finance their living expenses as well as tuition. My wife continued to work at her drug store job forty hours per week (sometimes more), and we still had to borrow the majority of our monthly budget.

What did chiropractic school cost me financially? The total amount which I had borrowed when I graduated was sixty-seven thousand dollars. My loans were a combination of Guaranteed Student Loans, which have a favorable rate of interest and do not accrue interest during the educational time, and Health Education Assistance Loans (HEAL), which do accrue interest while you are going to school, and whose rate of repayment is tied to the sale of US Treasury Bonds.

I had to defer the repayment of my loans many times in the early years because I simply was not making enough money to begin to pay them back. Deferment in either program means that the interest accrues on the unpaid balance, so that by the time that I was able to begin to pay the loans back, my principle amount had grown to about ninety thousand dollars. A minimum payment schedule would call for loan payments of about six hundred and fifty dollars per month. On this schedule, my GSL loans would be paid back in nineteen years, my HEAL loan in twenty-eight years. I would have paid over two hundred thousand dollars when they are both paid off.

It is not uncommon for me to hear now about students who borrow well over one hundred thousand dollars before they graduate from chiropractic school. I hate to think what their monthly payments will be, and how much they will actually pay back by the time the loans are satisfied.

Most people do not realize the financial commitment that it takes to become a chiropractor. I must admit that I did not consider this part of the commitment seriously enough. I encourage prospective students who have no savings and will have to borrow the entire loan amounts available to them through these programs to think seriously about their decision to become a chiropractor. The stress associated with this kind of debt is, in itself, enormous.

* * *

My practice was located in the heartland of the midwest. This meant that many, if not most, of my patients were farmers. I grew up in a small town rather than in the country; as a "town kid," I was hard pressed to tell you when corn was planted or when it was harvested. Thankfully, my dad had recently retired from a life-long career in the farm implement business, so I could always call him and ask what a combine was and other vital information needed for conversation with my farmer patients.

As you know, farmers have not had an easy time of it financially in the past years, and my patients were no exception. I listened for hours as they told me their troubles in a language I sometimes had a hard time deciphering.

I was positioning a rotund, ruddy-faced pig farmer for an x-ray one day, and he was telling me how bad things were financially. "I don't know how much it costs you "chiros" to get started," he offered, "but it's near impossible to keep a farm running today. Equipment is so expensive that we have to make do with what we have."

I wanted to tell him that the x-ray machine which was about to take his picture cost about twenty thousand dollars. I wanted to tell him that my chiropractic degree had cost me almost seventy thousand dollars. I wanted to tell him that my wife and I forbade our ten year old son from sledding that first winter because we couldn't yet afford health insurance for our family and we were afraid he'd break something.   Instead, I acted interested and sympathetic to his financial situation.

* * *

I have known students who had a good earning power, like nurses or pharmacists, to get through school with much less debt by working part time to help.  If they are solid students, working probably causes less stress than the nagging, constant worry over getting so far into debt caused me.

One cost that I could not have anticipated revolves around the central issue of this book - the misunderstanding of the chiropractic profession in the health care world.  This lack of understanding has limited opportunities for practicing chiropractors.  While medical doctors have several options including solo or group practice, associateship, employment by a hospital, research or academic medicine, the armed forces; chiropractors have only three options: become an associate doctor, stay at a chiropractic college as a resident or beginning teacher, or become involved in a solo practice.

Associating in an established practice is an option which every chiropractic student considers at one time or another.  Benefits of associating include learning from an established practitioner, incurring no more debt right away, and having a ready made panel of patients.   Most associateship positions that were available when I was close to graduating paid in the neighborhood of eighteen to twenty thousand dollars per year.  My last full year in the retail world, I had earned twenty-four thousand dollars.  It didn't seem possible that after all my education and all the money I had spent, that I would make less than I had earned before.  Even without paying back my loans, this salary would have made my family budget very tight;  but after adding in the school bills, living would have been impossible.  I was also concerned about finding the kind of practitioner  with whom I could work comfortably.  I had been trained to practice in quite a different way than many of the currently practicing chiropractors, and I was not willing to forget everything that I had learned just to have a job.  I don't know if graduates of other health professions see this same problem when they graduate, but as the science of chiropractic grows, there is an ever widening gap between how the new practitioners have been taught to practice and how the majority of the profession practices.  My generation of chiropractors are the first to have benefitted from a strong, scientifically-oriented curriculum.  For me, then associateship was an option that I did not pursue very aggressively.

The second option actually had a lot of appeal.  I had wanted to be a teacher ever since I could remember, but at the time I was a senior in high school there was a teacher glut in the midwest, and the guidance counselor at my high school discouraged me from pursuing teaching as a career.  I considered staying at Palmer and becoming a teacher, but ultimately didn't for two reasons.  The first was the salary.  Entry salaries were about the same as associating, and I felt that one of the reasons I had become a chiropractor was to enter the free market and make more money than I could as a retail manager.  Second, and most important, I had been trained to become a clinician.  I wanted to have an office of my own, treat patients, an use my new clinical judgement skills.  I talked with a chiropractor who had treated me, one who had taught at Palmer while he established his practice, and he encouraged me to go out and practice before I considered teaching.  Actually, this turned out to be good advice because the world of practice is so much different than the academic world.  I have found that students have more respect (rightfully so) for teachers who have made a living at practicing chiropractic than those who have never left the academic nest.

The third option was the one that I eventually chose. Instead of starting a practice from scratch, I bought an existing practice. I will not say that it was a poor choice, but it was definitely not a panacea for either my financial worries or for my search for a meaningful career. At the time that I graduated, the minimum figure being thrown around to begin a practice from "scratch" was about fifty thousand dollars. Now I hear educators talking about a figure more like seventy-five thousand dollars. Most of the students in my class, like myself, had no one to co-sign a loan that large: I remember many conversations about how we were going to convince a bank to loan us that kind of money with an unsecured loan. For many of us, the financial burden of starting a practice on top of our school loans seemed overwhelming.

My point here is this: opportunities for graduate chiropractors are slim when compared to the opportunities which exist for graduates of other health professions. Had I returned to school to be a nurse, I could have earned more money immediately than I could have as an associate chiropractor. Physical therapists in some parts of the country earn more than my chiropractic graduates can initially. Medical doctors and osteopaths can go to work in hospitals making large salary guarantees, with offices furnished and provided by the hospital. Group practices abound in the other health professions which would allow a new graduate to begin to practice with a minimum investment. These opportunities are especially important to the graduate who has had to borrow a lot of money just to get through school. Government programs like the National Health Service Corps, which assign a graduate health practitioner to a medically underserved area to work for a salary as well as forgiveness of his/her school loans have never included chiropractors in their program.  Chiropractic health care is still not considered a necessity in the US system.

* * *

What had I gained by going to school?  First, I held the hope of a stable financial future, being able to provide for my family in a better way than I could as a retail manager.  I had the hope of this future because I knew that as a licensed professional, I could go anywhere in the country to practice, and I expected that wonderful opportunities were out there.  I had a sense that the career that I had chosen was an important one, that I would have a greatly enhanced feeling of contributing to mankind as a Doctor of Chiropractic.  Retail management could never have given me such a sense of fulfillment.

Further, I was now a member of a profession.  Professions have the unmistakable feeling of a big fraternity which is important and comforting. I had never experienced membership in a group so strongly before, although I remember feeling something close when all the managers from JCPenney would get together at a meeting.  Association with people who do the same job as you brings a sense of belonging, of understanding, and camaraderie which works for us somehow.  I had that now with chiropractors across the country.

Last, I had gained academic degrees.  This was important to me since I had dropped out of college previously to get married.  I had always felt that I should have earned a bachelor's degree, but I hadn't.  I had read the short biographies of old friends solicited by high school reunion committees and felt jealous that I hadn't completed a degree.  Now I was armed with a B.S. in General Science and a Doctor of Chiropractic degree.  I had the feeling that

I had finally completed an educational process, and was proud of my degrees.

I also had a new name as a result of my education. From that day on, I have not been Mr. Boyer, but Dr. Boyer. I remember being acutely aware of my title when I first graduated. It was a feeling very similar to the feeling you have when you first get married. You want to show your ring to everyone and introduce your former girlfriend as "my wife." It is a feeling that you are different now than you were before. You view yourself differently and the world views you differently. Something about you has been changed fundamentally, and it is a change which is permanent. It must be similar to the feeling that women have if they take their husband's last name when they get married. I find that now the title has just become a part of me. When I call someone, or introduce myself, I call myself Dr. Boyer without giving it a second thought. For months, though, I remember thinking, "Should I say it's Dr. Boyer, or Kent Boyer?" I agonized over this because I didn't want to appear haughty or inappropriately formal, but I did want to display my accomplishment with pride. I had always been acutely aware that many people in and out of health care don't know what the appropriate title is for a chiropractor. I wanted to try to raise the consciousness of the public with regard to my profession.

There is something about being a chiropractor rather than a medical doctor or dentist which usually savvy people don't equate with the title doctor. We still get mail addressed to Mr. and Mrs. Boyer from even close relatives who certainly remember that I am a Doctor of Chiropractic. I often get mail addressed to Mr. Kent L. Boyer, DC, even from academic institutions who should be up on degrees and titles. What do people think the "D" stands for? The ultimate example of this kind of misunderstanding about title was several pieces of mail which I received from a chiropractic college addressed Mr.

Kent L. Boyer, DC!  You'd think that a chiropractic college employee would make the distinction.

This has never particularly bothered me personally, but I have found that one of the ways that self esteem can be taken away from a professional is to refuse to address the professional with the correct title.  I have seen it with members of many professions, and chiropractic is no exception.  I remember seeing Dr. Timothy Johnson (a medical doctor), ABC's medical correspondent and Ted Koppel discuss at length on Nightline whether a chiropractor should be called "doctor."  We call veterinarians  "doctor," for pete's sake, but the chiropractor should not be?

* * *

My wife works at a major university with a number of nursing faculty who have earned academic doctorate degrees.  She was told when typing correspondence for an interdisciplinary conference that only the medical doctors (and <u>not</u> the nurses with earned doctorates) were to be identified as "doctor."  One of the PhD faculty members recently received a piece of correspondence addressed to "Nurse Nancy Brown, PhD!"  Medical doctors do not hold the patent on the title doctor.

* * *

I hoped as a result of my education as a DC that I would gain a respectful career in life. First and foremost, I wanted to respect myself for what I had accomplished and what I did with my life.  Secondly, I think respect in the workplace is something we all want, whether we are a garbage collector or  politician or a health care professional.  We have created euphemisms for all kinds of occupations (my example above is a sanitary engineer) in our search for personal and occupational respect. I wanted that as much as everyone else.

I have always had a strong sense that I wanted my life to make a difference. Does every generation feel this way? I don't know. My generation, the lat of the baby-boomers coming into adulthood with Watergate may have somewhere gotten an extra dose of this desire for a purposeful career. No Wall Street for many of us, we are interested in purpose over money. I can't explain to you why I feel this way; in fact, at times it seeks stupid to me, but there it is.

I felt that health care was the way to go. I would have the respect of my patients, other providers, and the public for entering this philanthropic profession. I would also have a purposeful career which makes a difference in peoples lives.

As I entered practice that summer in 1987, there still were other things which I wanted to accomplish in my life. I wanted to continue to study for another graduate degree. I guess I knew right then that I was not always going to be satisfied just practicing chiropractic. I wanted to write. I started to fulfill that goal by writing newspaper columns (for which I was charged advertising rates) in my once-a-week local newspaper. I am now writing books.

I have previously mentioned that I wanted to teach. I knew even then that I wasn't interested in practice alone as a career goal. Most chiropractors don't feel the way that I did. Practicing for many is as fulfilling and exciting as the day they began. For all of us, the degree that we earned has been the beginning of an interesting yet sometimes frustrating experience.

* * *

The hierarchy of power which is the topic of this book has played a big role in my experience as a chiropractor. To a large degree, the future role of chiropractic in health care is dependent of the breakdown of this hierarchy and a rethinking of the way we perceive health care in this country.

# 2

# <u>What Is It That Chiropractors Do?</u>

I had been in chiropractic practice for less than a week. Because I had purchased an existing practice, I had a small base of patients who were used to coming to my office, and would probably continue unless they really couldn't stand me. I felt reasonably comfortable and "safe" with these patients - after all, they were "old hands" at this chiropractic stuff. What could they ask or expect of me that I couldn't answer or deliver?

The telephone rang, and I heard Norene, my wife and office manager, answer it. When she came back to my private office (actually a former dressing room), she was smiling. "Your first <u>new</u> patient is coming in at 11:00!" She was asking everyone who called for an appointment when they had last been in the office. If the caller was a former patient, we would look up their old file and I could get an idea of their previous history before I saw them. If the caller was a new patient, Norene would get a file ready for them.

This caller had replied that her husband had never been a patient before, so we had to anticipate what the problem could be. Norene got out all the color coded new patient information forms, and we waited. (Doctors new in practice seem to spend a lot of time waiting. For some reason, we don't want our patients to know this.)

A few minutes after 11:00, after the data forms had been filled out, she left the patient and his wife in the consultation room and came to get me. "Mr. Hall is ready for you now," she said. We were both excited for me to finally be out of school and seeing patients.

I opened the door to the room with some trepidation. I had had the same feeling when I had worked at a hospital years before as a nursing assistant. After I had been off for a weekend, I always felt a little pang of anxiety as I opened the door to a room of a patient whose name I didn't recognize to wake them up to take 7:30 vitals. I never knew what kind of health condition was behind that door. This felt the same way, a vaguely familiar anxiety. What I saw as I walked in surprised me.

I saw an emaciated, sick old man. Not "my low back hurts" or "I have a headache" sick, but "I should be in the hospital" sick. He was having a great deal of difficulty breathing. "What is he doing in my office?" I thought. I had been educated primarily to treat musculoskeletal conditions. I had heard about chiropractors treating all sorts of conditions with spinal manipulation, and had even read some research on the treatment of "organic" disorders with chiropractic care, but the bulk of my experience with these kinds of sick people came from my years in the hospital, where I wasn't in charge of their care. Most of my chiropractic college clinic patients had had musculoskeletal complaints.

"Good morning," I said, hoping to sound cheerful and confident, as I grabbed his file from the plexiglass holder outside the door. "I'm Dr. Boyer."

I looked quickly at the data sheet which asked the patient, among other questions, to write why they had come to the office that day. Mr. Hall had written "pneumonia."

Now I had seen plenty of patients who suffered from pneumonia when I worked in the hospital, and I could have guessed that the patient in front of me suffered from a respiratory pathology, but I guess I still expected to see the chief complaint blank filled in with the words "low back pain" or something.

"Tell me about your pneumonia, Mr. Hall."

"Doc, I just got out of the hospital yesterday. I've had emphysema for about ten years, but now I got pneumonia, too. I've never been to a chiropractor before, but I was hoping you could help me. I've got to get some relief so I can breathe easier. Will you take me?" he asked, working for every breath.

This was my first new patient experience. I'll never forget him.

* * *

Eight months later, it had become apparent to us that we needed a second telephone line into the clinic. Unfortunately, this was not possible until the telephone company did some digging and other expensive tasks. They would also have to do some work inside the office. We made an appointment with them for Thursday, the day we weren't normally in the office. I was to meet the men at 9:30 a.m. to let them in.

I walked over the single lane wooden railroad bridge between my house and office and arrived at the office at about 9:28. To my surprise, the telephone men were already working, and as I greeted them, I learned that they were ready to go inside to finish. Just as I was unlocking the door, a pick-up pulled into the parking lot and a middle-aged stranger got out.

I showed the telephone men where the phone cable came into the building and returned to the waiting room. "Can I help you?" I asked the stranger. I never knew what to say when I was alone in the office and a stranger came in. "Can I help you" sounded so retail, but I never came up with anything better.

"I need you to crack my back," he said simply. I should mention that I have always hated that phrase as a description of the health services that chiropractors perform. It makes the complicated job of diagnosis and treatment of joint dysfunction sound inanely simple and rough (which, by the way, it is not.) However, this is the way many of my patients talked, so I translated his statement in my mind to mean that he wanted to be evaluated as a new patient.

I guess I must have hesitated for a minute, because he broke into my thoughts. "I have seen the other chiropractor, the one who used to be here."

"How long ago was that?" I asked, in order to know where to look for his file.

"Oh, a couple of years ago now," he replied, a "what's-the-difference" look coming over his face.

I told him I would go to the storage room and get his file, and asked him to have a seat in the empty waiting room. I was not overly surprised when I found in his file that his previous single visit to my office had been nine years before!

I took a deep breath and expelled it in a long sigh, then walked back toward the waiting room to explain for perhaps the hundredth time the way in which I practiced. I would have to perform an examination, perhaps including x-rays of his area of complaint. Only after this diagnostic examination, could I determine if his problem required an adjustment or some other type of treatment. I was beginning to sound like a broken record to the myriad of patients who had never heard of anything like this from a chiropractor. They were used to being questioned briefly, then adjusted. Not much diagnostic work, no choices in treatment. In and out.

The explanation completed, the stranger whined, "But you don't understand... Every so often, I get this catch in my back, and all I need is a crack and it's fine again."

And so the patients came, at one of these two extremes, sick with any number of diseases, or with a problem commonly self-diagnosed as a "catch" in their back or neck. Many presented somewhere in between. Some had problems which I felt I could treat, others had to be referred to another type of provider. Referrals to me from other doctors were few.

* * *

I feel that I left chiropractic college well trained to diagnose and treat patients safely and effectively. I feel that I knew what I, as a chiropractor, could treat and when I needed to refer the patient to another type of provider. I was not prepared, however, for the great misunderstanding that I found in patients and other health care providers about what chiropractic science is, and what chiropractors do.

Chiropractic medicine is greatly misunderstood. Public awareness and perception of chiropractic health care is probably the profession's major problem. In most cases, I just don't think chiropractors know what to do to correct these misconceptions. These issues of awareness and perception are, at the same time, both the profession's greatest liability and it's greatest opportunity.

Why the big misunderstanding? First, awareness of chiropractic is much higher in some locations than in others. There are also a great deal of differences in how chiropractors practice. Some have a very narrow scope of what they treat and the services they perform, and others have very broad, general practices. Unlike many other professions, when the practitioner was educated makes a big difference in how he or she practices. Chiropractic education has undergone an extreme metamorphosis in the past two decades. Chiropractic education was quite parochial before accreditation (1973), so that where a particular chiropractor was educated prior to accreditation makes an enormous difference in how he or she practices. The more recent graduates were educated under more stringent scientific guidelines than those educated some years ago. I can't imagine another profession which has upgraded internally as much as chiropractic has in the past several decades. While this improvement is desirable and necessary, it has created a dichotomy between practicing chiropractors which will take a generation to go away.

I have found that geography has a great deal to do with patient's perception of what a chiropractor does. I am certain that I saw many varied conditions in my office because I practiced in Iowa, chiropractic's home state. In Iowa, public awareness of the chiropractic profession is high and has a long history. I treated patients who had been seeing a chiropractor for fifty years. I treated people who had been chiropractic patients since infancy; their parents and grandparents were patients of mine, too. One patient, a woman born the same year I was, had a tattered file which was entitled "Baby Diane." Her first visit had been three weeks after birth; her chief complaint on that visit according to her mother was colic. Even today, almost one hundred years after the founding of chiropractic by D.D. Palmer in Davenport, it is difficult to locate a town in Iowa with a population of one thousand or more which doesn't have a chiropractic office. New graduates of the profession's founding school (now Palmer Chiropractic University, still in Davenport) populated Iowa years ago. In many of these small towns, the chiropractor was and is the only doctor of any type.

This level of awareness of the chiropractic profession is not found all across the country. While there are, like Iowa, states which also have a long history of chiropractic health care, some locales still have cities and entire counties which do not have a chiropractic office. Awareness about chiropractic is lower in these areas because the chiropractor is not an accessible health choice. Chiropractic health care is certainly not as ubiquitous or universal as traditional medical care.

The high level of awareness and the generally favorable public perception in Iowa has not, however, resulted in a clear understanding of the role of the chiropractor in these patient's health care. As my two examples above show, the range of perception was from "chiropractors just crack backs" all the way to "chiropractors treat any health problem." Which is right?

* * *

The answer to the question is that chiropractors practice in many different ways. Let me describe for you the broadest scope of practice which is currently taught in accredited chiropractic colleges.

In the broadest scope of practice, a chiropractor is a primary care physician who treats human ailments without prescription drugs or surgery. Primary care means that the patient makes an appointment directly with the provider rather than going through another doctor. The broad scope chiropractor is equipped to see any kind of non-emergency health problem, make an initial diagnosis, and then treat the patient or refer him to another kind of doctor for further diagnosis and/or treatment if that doctor is more appropriate.

While a broad scope chiropractor is often criticized by the medical profession or media as being unaware of his professional limitations, in actuality, this is how our students are educated. Chiropractic students take courses and national examinations in general diagnosis, obstetrics and gynecology, cardiovascular pathology, and emergency procedures, just to name a few. The idea of this broad scope model is not to treat every patient who walks through the chiropractor's door, but to function as a primary care or portal of entry provider. In order to be a safe practitioner, a chiropractor must know how to diagnose enough conditions to know when to treat the patient and when to refer. Since I practiced as a broad scope chiropractor, let me explain how this might work. I didn't ever turn a potential patient over to another doctor until I knew what was wrong with them and had ascertained that I couldn't help them. Here's an example.

A high school student athlete whom I had treated previously was sent by his parents to see me after he fell and hurt his ankle. The injury had just occurred and the ankle was swelling rapidly. I thought there was a possibility that the boy's ankle was broken. Instead of sending him to the MD's office in case it was broken, I x-rayed it myself. Chiropractors actually have more training in reading x-rays than any other health professional except radiologists. They are fully qualified to take and read x-rays and to diagnose fractures. As it turned out, the boy's ankle was not fractured, but severely sprained. I proceeded to treat him for a sprained ankle. (Research has shown that chiropractors treat sprains and strains with more cost effectiveness and the patients return to their daily activities quicker than with either medical or osteopathic care.) So I had spared the boy from an unnecessary office visit to the medical doctor because his condition was one which I was able to treat.

In another case, I may do lab work and determine that my patient has a bacterial infection. This patient would be sent off to the medical doctor for antibiotics. Practicing as a broad scope chiropractor does not mean that the chiropractor has a disdain for medications when necessary. In fact, I have found that broad scope practitioners are probably less likely to want to practice in the isolation which used to surround chiropractors. They are more likely to have developed a network of other providers with whom they work. A primary health care provider, then, diagnoses each patient with the intention of treating the patient or referring the patient to the appropriate provider.

In most states, chiropractors have full diagnostic rights. This means that they are licensed to do physical examinations including listening to hearts and breath sounds, looking in eyes and ears, taking vital signs and doing orthopedic and neurologic tests. I took my own x-rays, could order CT scans or MRI studies, took blood and urine samples and sent them to a lab via the same courier who serviced the medical clinic and hospital. I was fully and adequately trained to do this. In addition, I did functional evaluations of the patient's spine and other joints, evaluated gait and soft tissue changes. If any of the physical exam findings required treatment which was beyond my treatment scope (the patient needed hospitalization, drugs, surgery or a fracture set), I referred them to a carefully chosen network of other doctors.

In the treatment realm, many chiropractors do much more than just adjust or manipulate (synonymous terms) the spine. I did some nutritional and dietary counseling; used physical modalities such as ice, heat, traction, and ultrasound; designed and recommended exercise and rehabilitation programs; used orthotics like cervical pillows and collars, lumbar supports, heel lifts, and taped or wrapped strained joints. I cleaned out patient's ear canals, ordered canes, walkers, and crutches when necessary, and manipulated the spine and extremity joints. I had been trained to use all of these procedures in chiropractic college and post-graduate courses.

The chiropractors who had owned my practice before did only the chiropractic exams and adjusted patients. That's it. This is the narrowest scope of practice. As you can see, there is quite a bit of difference between the two. Quite often, I found myself explaining at length to patients the need for the services I provided.

The majority of my practice was spine and other joint disorders. However, I loved the other types of cases because I was able to use the other skills I had learned in school, and in many cases, I was able to help the patient get better without drugs or surgery. You might be surprised what positive health results you can get for many conditions using the conservative methods I have described above. I often thought about ancient or isolated civilizations who got along quite well without all of our modern pharmacopeia. With the plethora of side effects possible, I think it is wise to do everything that can be done before turning to prescription drugs. Chiropractors are trained to correct causes when possible rather than masking or dulling symptoms with medication.

* * *

One day in high school gym class, I heard a pop and felt pain in the center of my chest while "walking" with my arms across parallel bars. When the pain didn't go away after a few days, my parents took me to the medical doctor. He asked me briefly about the injury and prescribed Valium. It helped temporarily, but I had the pain off and on for years afterward. One day years later when I was in a chiropractor's office, I asked him to look at my chest. He explained that the ribs form a joint with the sternum (breastbone) and that if that joint becomes dysfunctional or unable to move, pain can occur. He adjusted the joint with his hands and a day later, I was pain free. This story illustrates this different philosophy between the two professions. In retrospect, it is probably not a wise idea to give high school kids Valium.

* * *

Most patients don't realize that many types of so-called organic diseases have a spinal joint dysfunction accompanying them. Take asthma for instance. Asthma can have many different causes. It can be related to stress, related to airborne allergies, food allergies, lung pathologies, or related to the spinal and rib joint dysfunctions. If the patient has a kind of asthma which is related to the spine or spinal nerves, the best doctor that patient could see is a chiropractor. This is where the public gets confused. They think that all diseases except back pain should be treated by a medical doctor, because they don't understand what chiropractors do. They hear that a patient is being treated by a chiropractor for asthma, and they think that the chiropractors claim they can treat anything, without limitations. This is not the case at all. In fact, no doctor, no matter what his initials, can successfully treat every case which crosses his threshold.

Chiropractors would like the public to think that they are very united with regard to what a chiropractor should do, what he/she should treat, and how to do this. Unfortunately, this is not true. Chiropractors cannot agree. Fortunately, there is (in my perception anyway) a clear majority consensus for the scope issue, and that majority agrees that chiropractors should function as they are educated, as primary care doctors.

* * *

The distribution between broad and narrow scopes of practice among chiropractors is an important one. One afternoon while I was still in chiropractic college, the telephone rang. I was alone in our mobile home studying, so I got up to answer the phone by our bed.

"Kent?  I need some advice."  It was Les, my best friend from my early college years, now teaching band in Denver.  He didn't sound like his usual jolly self.

"What's the matter?"  I asked.

"Well, I woke up this morning, and I can hardly walk.  My low back is killing me.  What should I do?"

Definitely not my normal conversation with my kooky friend.  I thought for a minute.  Of course, I thought he should go to a chiropractor, but who?  I wanted to recommend a chiropractor who was a careful diagnostician, who used a variety of approaches to his/her care, who would treat Les like I would.  How to find that?  Look in the yellow pages?  Then what?  Pick the office with the biggest, flashiest ad, or the single line listing of the office nearest you?

"I haven't hung up on you, I'm just thinking," I stalled.  "First, do you know anyone who you teach with who goes to a chiropractor?  Ask them if their chiropractor took an x-ray of them when they first went.  Ask them if he/she did tests to figure out what caused the problem.  Ask them if the chiropractor does anything besides adjusting them."  I was on a roll now.  But what if he couldn't find a fellow teacher who sees a chiropractor?

* * *


How should a prospective patient find out how an individual chiropractor practices?  Ask the receptionist if the chiropractor does physical therapy or blood tests.  Ask if the chiropractor will refer you to another type of doctor if that is appropriate for your case.  Ask if the chiropractor can help you with your nutritional or dietary questions.  If the answer to these questions is yes, you are talking to a broad scope chiropractic office.  Your particular health needs will dictate whether you require a broad or narrow scope chiropractic office. For example, if your health problem is a backache or headache, either a broad or narrow scope chiropractor would be fine. But if you want more generalized office based health care, seek a broad scope office.

The largest national chiropractic association, the American Chiropractic Association (ACA), recently asked its members what types of conditions they treat. These chiropractors said that eighty-five percent of their patient visits are related to the musculoskeletal system. Low back pain, headache, neck pain or an extremity joint problem, like knee pain, could all be considered musculoskeletal complaints. Nine percent of the survey respondent's visits are for visceromotor conditions. These are disorders which are related to the organs (viscera) of the body, such as asthma, ulcers, diarrhea/constipation, and the like. Four percent of the patient visits to chiropractors were of a vascular nature, such as poor circulation in the hands or feet, and two percent were for "other" types of problems as well as physicals and general examinations. I guess from this information we could conclude that what most chiropractors treat most often is musculoskeletal disorders. But they do also routinely see patients for other types of conditions. These figures also suggest that while chiropractic students are taught to be generalists, many patients still think of chiropractors as musculoskeletal doctors.

Much of the disparity over how chiropractors practice has to do with which college the chiropractor had attended and when he/she was educated. Chiropractic health care was originally taught as a complete alternative to traditional allopathic medicine. Chiropractors proclaimed with a religious zeal that adjustments alone should be used for all possible health conditions, from birth to death. The theory was that joint dysfunction (then called subluxations) caused all disease.  Some schools perpetuated  this overstated utilization theory longer than others. Certain schools recognized early on that as a limited scope practice (no drugs or surgery), chiropractors should think of themselves as part of a health team, even if they might be the patient's primary doctor.  This is one of the reasons that practicing chiropractors vary so much in their scope of practice:  the schools didn't agree on this until recently.

Even today, some schools emphasize treatment of musculoskeletal conditions only while others emphasize the broader scope.  However, accreditation has made the schools much less parochial.  The newer graduates are a more united breed of practitioner.

For most of the profession's history, chiropractic students have been taught with anecdote or using empirical evidence.  This means that clinical phenomenon seen in chiropractic practices was used as the authority for teaching.  Since chiropractors have only been involved in scientific research for the past fifteen years, what could have been used in the colleges before that as authority? Anecdote. Modern chiropractic education, like other health professions, still uses anecdote or empirical evidence of health benefits from treatment.  However, the more recent graduates have had the added benefit of clinical trials and scientific literature in addition to the empirical based training.  Due to recent research, chiropractors have begun to re-think and question everything which used to be taken for granted in chiropractic education.  Surprisingly, much of the research into basic chiropractic tenets has proven historical theories to be correct.  This research and upgrading to a true science has resulted in much better diagnostic skills, too.  Before research, many of the teachers were in part time private practice, or had practiced full time at some time in their careers, and they taught what they had seen in their practices.  The student, therefore, could come out of a school having been taught by Dr. X, who treated condition A with treatment B. If instead, the student had Dr. Y for that class, he might say that you treat condition A with treatment C. Without any clinical studies in the profession, as well as a strong disrespect and suspicion of medical and osteopathic research, you can see why the educational process perpetuated this confusion. Every teacher had his or her own theory about what chiropractic was, and these ideas couldn't be refuted because there had been no research done to compare the efficacy of treatments.

* * *

My friend Joe treated a young mother in the college clinic where we went to school. She had gotten such good relief from her headaches that she asked Joe to evaluate her toddler, who had recurrent tonsillitis. Joe had been telling her about research he had read regarding children and tonsillitis. The group of children being studied (by German medical doctors who do manipulation) were all chronic sufferers of upper respiratory infections (URI). The researchers found that a large number of these kids had upper cervical (neck) joint dysfunction, which responded well to manipulatory treatment. They followed the children for a couple of years to find that the manipulation was more helpful in controlling URI than the previously prescribed antibiotics.

Joe had worked the child up, and now needed a signature from a staff doctor before the patient could check out at the front desk. The only staff doctor readily available was Dr. Smith, a chiropractor who made no secret of his personal belief that chiropractors should only treat back pain. The diagnostic code that Joe had used for the child was 474.0, tonsillitis.

Dr. Smith took a look at the form and laughed in a condescending way. "Chiropractors don't treat tonsillitis!" he laughed. "Change this to a musculoskeletal code and I'll sign it."

Joe was furious. He decided that it wasn't worth arguing with this guy, who had obviously decided that his opinion of chiropractic was the only one which mattered. Instead, Joe took the form to another chiropractor who was aware of the research. She signed the form and told Joe he was doing a good job.

* * *

When patients have been taught about chiropractic by a practitioner who has been educated in a different era, their understanding of what chiropractic is about is quite different than the newer model.

Along comes a new practitioner like me. I want to change all the old ideas about chiropractic and base my practice on science. I am suspicious of all the anecdotal stores I have heard. And I want to teach my patients based on science.

* * *

I had treated Jane for a variety of musculoskeletal conditions, most recently for headaches which seemed to be stress related. Jane had five kids under the age of eight, and she and her husband were starting their own business.

One day, I came into the treatment room to find Jane highly agitated. I had not seen her for a month, and had assumed that she was doing well.

"Feel my low back and tell me what you think," she said. Not following her, I asked, "Has your low back been bothering you?"

"No," she said, "I'm afraid I'm pregnant."

Now I was really lost. She continued, "I wanted you to feel my back and tell me if I'm pregnant or not. Dr. Hall (the previous chiropractor) was the one who diagnosed my other five pregnancies by feeling my back."

I must have missed something in school. I could have sworn that pregnancy diagnosis was done with a urine test. As many unusual stories as I had heard about special chiropractic diagnosis, this was a new one. How was I to tell Jane that I didn't possess this skill, and as far as I knew, the idea was ridiculous, and still maintain my appearance of competence?

* * *

Individual chiropractors through the years have educated patients, then, about their services with the information that has been available to them as students. Since much of the treatment protocol was taught by clinicians using only anecdotal evidence from their own practices, in certain schools, chiropractic students were taught to treat such conditions as infertility, bedwetting, and excema with adjustments. Little was taught about the treatment of these types of conditions when I was in college, so I was often surprised when patients presented in my office asking me to help them with these complaints. Obviously, someone had told them about positive results for these types of conditions with a chiropractor.

In retrospect, I was not always right about my perceived inability to treat some conditions with chiropractic adjustments. My patients had often experienced clinical results for conditions I wasn't so sure could be treated with chiropractic care. I became more respectful of their anecdotal stories as

I practiced. There are many consequences of joint dysfunction which are still not understood or well researched. There is still much to be learned. Admitting that does not weaken the profession, but instead opens new avenues of exploration.

* * *

I drove into my office parking lot one morning to find a rusty, mustard yellow Ford Torino backed in to the space nearest the door. As I got out of my car and walked toward the door, a feeble elderly man in overalls got out of the Ford.

"Howdy, doc," he offered politely. "Can you see me this morning?"

"Let's check the appointment book," I said, turning the key in the lock. These patients rarely used the telephone to make appointments. The chiropractor's office had been like a barber shop: you sat in the waiting room until it was your turn. Since the only doctor-patient encounters which had ever taken place there were x-rays and adjustments, nobody had ever had to wait long. I was doing physical exams, long consultations and other types of treatment in addition to adjustments. Appointments were necessary.

As it turned out, I could see him then. I proceeded to listen to his chief complaint of a six day bout with being unable to move his bowels. What was I to do about this? I knew of no studies relating chiropractic to regular bowel movements. I explained to the patient my misgivings, which he dismissed with the wave of a hand.

"A good adjustment has always worked before," he said cheerfully.

To make a long story short, I gave him several natural dietary and activity strategies for relieving constipation, but also found a dysfunctional joint in his low back. After assessing that he could be safely manipulated, I performed a lumbar spine adjustment. Then came the lecture.

"I want to see you tomorrow," I began. "An impacted bowel can be a serious matter which shouldn't be ignored." I hoped that the dietary changes and exercise I had told him to do would take care of the problem. But I wasn't going to take any chances.

Later that day, Norene came into the consulting room where I was reading an x-ray. "Mr. Jones from this morning is on the telephone," she said. I picked up the extension.

"Doc? This is Jones talking. Just wanted to let you know that my bowels moved about an hour ago. Looks like I won't need to drive into town to see you tomorrow. You did good by me, son. Appreciate it."

I stood there with my mouth open looking at the receiver. Coincidence? Magic? Luck? What was the physiological explanation? This wouldn't be the only time that a patient's response to treatment left me speechless.

* * *

Ellen had worked for Dr. Hall as his receptionist when he owned my office previously. She was now a cook in the local nursing home, one of the town's largest employers. Her low back had been bothering her.

Ellen was one of those patients who I enjoyed seeing. She was pleasant and complimentary about the way I ran my office. After I had done a good diagnostic work up on her, I began to treat her with manipulation and therapy. She was beginning to do better.

One day, when I walked into the treatment room, she said, "I'm mad at you."

What had I done to make her mad?   "Why?" I asked.

"Well, you know that my youngest son is ten.  I haven't had a regular period since he was born, and I had kind of gotten used to that.  In the three months that you have been working on my low back, I have begun to have a period every twenty-eight days.  So I'm mad at you," she explained, clearly joking.

I was speechless.   I had not even known about her menstrual irregularity, and I certainly had not been treating her for it.  But, apparently, by working with the joints of her low back, her body had been stimulated to a regular cycle again.  Amazing.

This phenomenon  occasionally happens in traditional  medicine, too.  Remember  a few years ago when the medical community found by accident that the drug Minoxydil, which was being used to treat hypertension, also stimulated  hair growth in certain  bald men?

* * *

So a new practitioner  of chiropractic  is often at a loss when discussing conditions which an older practitioner  routinely treated  successfully, given the absence of case studies or clinical trials in the literature.  In chiropractic, since clinical  studies  have  only  existed  for  the  past  couple  decades,  new practitioners  sometimes begin to feel that the patient  knows something  they don't.  To carry this idea to the extreme, many long-time chiropractic patients have gotten the idea, either as a result of a chiropractor  or as a result of their own wishful thinking, that there is an adjustment  for virtually everything.  This misunderstanding  can lead to patient  expectations  which are too high and much trepidation  for the new chiropractor.

* * *

I remember  a soft spoken, sweet old lady who had been  a chiropractic patient  for at least forty years.  She and her husband  continued  to visit me every couple of weeks for manipulation,  due mainly to arthritic pain which the adjustments  alleviated  for a time.  This woman visited me one winter day and said, "My throat  has been  so dry.  Can you adjust me for that?"  I didn't know how to respond  to her question.   One the one hand, if I said what I wanted to say ("of course not!"), the patient  would think either  I didn't know what I was  talking  about  (particularly  if a previous DC had  told  her  adjustments would help her with that condition),  or she would feel stupid having asked and may not tell me what was bothering her  in the future.  Patients often don't mention  health  concerns  which they feel are unrelated  to the type of doctor they are seeing at the time.

Feeling that the best approach  with a patient  was always the truth (as I knew it), I proceeded  to explain  that while there  wasn't an adjustment  for a dry throat, I could give her some advice on how to get through  the winter without being bothered  by it. I proceeded  to explain to her about dry, heated air and villi and mucous, the importance  of humidity in the house in the winter and drinking plenty of fluids.  I explained  more to her than I am sure she wanted to know about why her throat felt dry.  After all, she just wanted an adjustment  for it!

* * *

Imagine the quandary  of the newly graduated  chiropractor  who tries to correct these misconceptions  for a longtime patient.   "The science of chiropractic  has advanced  since Dr. X was graduated," the new chiropractor might try.  "Dr. X was using the explanation  which was known at the time he was in school..." Or, "We are now taught..." In the end, the new chiropractor may choose to go along with the outdated  model just to avoid the controversy, the result being that the antiquated  model is perpetuated.

I wondered  several  times  if I was  the only newly  graduated  DC who was having this problem. I had scheduled a "patient appreciation  day" for my patients.  My friend, Dr. Carol Adams and I had decided  that we would help each  other  on  a  special  day,  and  have  our  patients  bring  food  for  the upcoming  holiday  season  instead  of paying  for services  that day.  The food that I collected  was to be donated  to the food bank run by the churches  in my town.

Carol  was  going  to  see  all of the new  patients  for me,  taking  histories, doing  examinations,  and  taking  x-rays if necessary.  I was going  to be busy treating  existing patients.  All of the services were free.  I liked  the idea of a patient  without  health  insurance  being  able to get his/her  diagnostic  services by donating  some cans of food.  I thought  maybe I would do this a couple  of times a year.

(Before  I tell you  the rest  of the  story, I must  tell  you about  the first patient of the day.  LeRoy  was an existing patient  who was always talking about how bad times were for farmers like him.  To my surprise, he walked in to the clinic for his free appointment  with a huge box full of food.  "My daughter and her husband  had some hard times once and the food bank came to their rescue," he explained.  I knew then  that the day was going to be a success.)

Annette,  the  adult  daughter  of a patient  of mine  had  called  for an appointment  on the patient appreciation  day.  I knew from her mother that Annette  was the patient of a chiropractor  in another  town.  Annette  had also requested that her daughter be seen, a little mite who had trouble with asthma.

I was treating regular patients in the two treatment rooms I had. As I left one room to go to the other, I saw Carol coming out of the consultation room, where she was working with the new patients.

"Kent," she called, "Annette Jackson is in the consulting room. She's really upset that she waited in the waiting room so long and she isn't going to get treated today." The new patients who had been through the diagnostic work-up on the free day were to be rescheduled for another day for a report of findings visit. On this visit, I would explain what Carol and I had found after we had correlated all the information that Carol was gathering for me.

"She also refuses x-rays, even though her chief complaint is neck pain following a car accident several years ago. She says that a Dr. Dower has treated her all of these years without x-rays, so why should she get them now? I think she's got some arthritis in her neck. What do you want me to do?"

We had agreed on the procedure that we would follow, and I knew that Carol would make about the same diagnostic judgements that I would. If there was a question about what should be done, I had told her to come and see me.

I couldn't believe that a patient was arguing with Carol when she was getting the services free. I really didn't have time that day to give lengthy explanations to patients that day, and I was tempted just to tell Carol to ask her to leave.

Instead, I went into the consult room to try to explain why we needed the exam and x-ray and why it would take me some time to review all the information and talk with Carol and reschedule her so I could talk with her about her health before she could safely be treated. I found Annette to be hostile and indignant, her attitude threatening to ruin the festive mood of my "community service" day.

It was obvious that I was not going to be able to explain the procedures to her logically, her mind was made up. I remember Carol saying that chiropractors used to be trained just to do adjustments, but now our training was much better, and we were interested in making a diagnosis and finding the cause of her problem. I knew then that Carol had had this same conversation with many of her patients who were also used to seeing an older practitioner.

Annette left in a huff, refusing our free services. The day, however, was a success, and we donated two car trunkfuls of food and over $100 in cash to the food bank. A week later, our picture was on the front page of the weekly newspaper. I wondered what Annette thought when she saw it.

* * *

Even in the back pain realm, the area which has been most researched, patients often think that their encounter with the chiropractor of the 1950s for a back ache will be similar forty years later. Patients expect medicine to have advanced with new diagnostic equipment and techniques. For some reason, the same expectation is not applied to chiropractic. Many patients were lead to believe that DCs exist to crack or pop their spine "back into place" once a year or so when they develop a pain. They scorn the idea of physical examinations, lab work, or radiologic examinations to diagnose their conditions because the previous chiropractor didn't use these procedures. They also scorn the idea of returning to the chiropractor for follow up care. They have been educated to expect a miracle result with one adjustment or to be managed by the chiropractor saying, "Come back when it hurts again."

This was apparently  the problem  with the man  who wanted  his "back cracked" above.  What he expected  was to be laid down on the table after he showed me where the pain was, to be adjusted, and to be relieved  of the pain. What  he got  instead  was a modern  chiropractor  who realized  that the pain could be a result of many things.  What he didn't seem  to understand  was that I needed  to diagnose  why he had  the pain  before  I could  recommend  a treatment  program.


* * *


One cool fall afternoon  I was in the treatment  room  with Ruth  Cooper. My wife knocked  on the door, opened  it, and apologized  for interrupting  us. I stepped  out into the hall and my wife said, "There is a woman on the phone who is having neck pain.  She has been  x-rayed at the  medical clinic and they said her x-rays are normal.  She wants to know if you will require  x-rays in order  to treat  her?"

I told  my wife to have  the lady pick  up her  x-rays at the  clinic and bring them  in with her so I would  not have  to repeat  the x-rays.

When  I stepped  back into the treatment  room, Mrs. Cooper  admitted that she had overheard  the conversation.   "How does she expect you to know what's wrong with her if you take another  doctor's word for it that everything is normal?"

I couldn't  help but smile to myself.  I had  done a good job explaining my role  and practice  style  to Mrs. Cooper.


* * *

Patients should expect to improve unless they have been diagnosed to have a chronic condition and can only expect temporary relief. In the absence of improvement after a reasonable amount of time, the patient should begin to ask questions about further diagnostic tests, referral to another type of doctor, or some other plan.

Any doctor who wants you to begin treatment without doing any diagnostic tests is not practicing in a safe way. Even a simple health problem deserves more than a cursory thirty second examination. All types of doctors can be guilty of this.

Walt, a seventy-five year old farmer came to see me after he had been to the medical doctor. "Doctor Green says I have bursitis in my shoulder, but the pills he gave me haven't helped much. Do you think that you could give me some relief?"

I had become used to seeing patients after they had been elsewhere for help and had been unsatisfied with the results. What I found difficult was explaining to the patient that my license to practice as a doctor of chiropractic gave me both the right and responsibility to diagnose their problem myself, rather than to accept another doctor's diagnosis. This seemed especially true if the patient had not improved after being treated by the other doctor. This does not mean that doctors should not share test results to avoid duplication of services. But the treating doctor has the responsibility to interpret the test results before designing treatment.

"How did Dr. Green diagnose your bursitis?" I asked.

Walt looked at me incredulously, not realizing what I was asking. "Well, I described the pain to him and showed him where it hurt," he began, pointing to his shoulder, "and he said it was bursitis."

Walt surprised me. When I explained to him what I needed to do to accurately differentiate between bursitis and the many other conditions which could cause shoulder pain, he said, "Let's get to it, doc." If all patients could follow my logic about diagnosis, I thought, I would have it made.

* * *

Similar conditions do not always respond the same to chiropractic treatment. Many predisposing factors are involved in the patient's response. The patient's age, previous health, nutrition, compliance with home care, and desire to improve all can impact the result of the treatment.

Ralph was an eighty-two year old bachelor farmer who still had some livestock. He had slipped and fallen on the ice when he was out feeding his chickens, and was in extreme pain. The injury had occurred about a week before his "lady friend" Gertrude called me late one afternoon. "I think I can get him to come now if you will wait for us," she said. We waited.

I could see that Ralph was in a lot of pain as he slowly walked into the waiting room. The first thing I wanted to do was to take an x-ray to rule out a fracture. Ralph was shaking from the effort of walking, so my wife and I stood him in front of the x-ray machine, and began to help him into a patient gown. When I lifted up his shirt, I found an ancient Ace bandage wrapped loosely around his abdomen. "I thought if I wrapped it, my back would feel better," he whispered sheepishly.

I unwound him like a mummy, and took the x-rays I needed. Ralph had a severely degenerated and osteoporotic lumbar spine, and one of his lumbar vertebrae had collapsed due to the fall.

Now I had to make a decision. If I sent him to a medical doctor, I felt sure that Ralph would be put in a hospital (mainly to make sure that he would rest.) I had worked in a hospital long enough to know that if they took Ralph's clothes and put him into a hospital gown, took his glasses and his dentures, and made him lay in bed all day that it was probable that he would lose his spirit, eventually lose himself, and possibly end up in a nursing home. But it was also my responsibility to provide the best and safest care that I could for him. I weighed my choices.

I decided to have a private talk with Gertrude. "Can Ralph stay with you for a while?" I asked. I knew that this was unusual, but Ralph clearly couldn't be alone. Gertrude's virtue as a single woman aside, I thought if he could stay with her, I could safely treat him rather than refer him.

She didn't hesitate for a minute. "Of course," she replied, "I'll make him understand." She had intuitively known how serious the problem was.

Ralph made a remarkable recovery. In a couple of weeks he was much improved, and (reluctantly, I think) had moved back into his farmhouse. His worst complaint by then was that he was constipated. I gave him suggestions on increasing fiber in his diet, had him force fluids, and rock in a rocking chair. This took care of that problem, and his back was feeling much better, too. By spring, his injuries had healed enough that he was back to normal.

* * *

Several months later, a woman called to make an appointment for the widower that she kept house for. He had fallen in the bathtub, and was having pain and difficulty walking.

This patient's x-ray looked similar to Ralph's. He didn't appear to be in nearly the same previous health though. He had used a walker for several years, and was much more helpless than Ralph.

Once again, the problem of whether to attempt to manage the patient, or to refer? I talked in confidence to the housekeeper. "I am going to work with Mr. Hutsinger every day for a few days, and watch him carefully. I might have to refer him to his medical doctor and I'm afraid he might have to go to the hospital.

"That's what he is so afraid of, Doctor. I think that's why he insisted that I call you in the first place."

The next day, Mr. Hutsinger was actually smiling when he shuffled into the office with the housekeeper behind him. "I'm walking a lot better, doc," he beamed. I had to agree, he seemed improved. I treated him and turned to his friend. "Let's see you again tomorrow," I said. "We need to work very aggressively on this."

The next day, Mr. Hutsinger was in much more pain than on the day I first saw him. His walking was worse. It was time to refer him. I needed to see at least a little improvement each visit, or I felt I was withholding an appropriate referral.

Tears welled up in his eyes when I told him I was going to call the local medical doctor and see if he could be seen at once. "I don't want to be stuck in a nursing home, doc."

It was pathetic. I understood, but he needed twenty-four hour a day care right now, and that was more than the loyal housekeeper could be expected to do. As I suspected, Mr. Hutsinger entered the hospital that day. A week later, I read in the newspaper that he had died.

Had I betrayed Mr. Hutsinger? Would he have eventually improved if I had seen him for a while more? I'll never know. I had done for him what I felt was best.

* * *

What do chiropractors do?

Chiropractors are trained to diagnose and treat more health problems than most people realize. While the majority of the conditions they treat relate to the joints of the body, you might be surprised to find how well trained your chiropractor is in other disorders.

When I was a hospital orderly, I was assigned to take care of a terminal cancer patient who also had a grossly disfiguring case of neurofibromatosis. Her body was covered with clusters of grape-like tumors which must have made her life a living hell. I read everything I could find on this horrible, rare disease. Later, in chiropractic college, we learned about neurofibromatosis in pathology class and I recalled my hospital patient.

Soon after I had started practicing, one of my first patients was the mother of a little girl, Allison, who also has neurofibromatosis. Allison suffered from debilitating headaches which made her vomit. In the course of treating Allison's mother, we discussed at length her daughter's diagnosis and their frequent trips to the University of Iowa for evaluation. On her next trip to Iowa City, Allison's mom proudly told her doctors that her new chiropractor knew more about neurofibromatosis than her family physicians. She was relieved to have found some help for Allison's headaches, too.

Chiropractors are not poorly trained or frustrated medical doctors. They are well educated generalists who have a special interest in the ramifications of neuromusculoskeletal dysfunction. These dysfunctions most likely express themselves in joint and muscle pain, but can also cause other types of health problems.

Early chiropractors were often radical anti-medical isolationists. This description no longer fits the modern DC, who is well aware of his/her role in the scheme of things. The modern chiropractor sees him/herself as a member of a health care team - sometimes the health manager for a particular patient, sometime a doctor to whom a patient has been referred. Patients should be free to make a choice as to who their health manager is.

The misunderstanding about what chiropractors do is very frustrating to everyone - patients, other health providers, and especially to chiropractors themselves.

The theory of science and scientific knowledge allows for a continuing and widening spiral of information. As questions are asked and answered by curious researchers, new questions arise. Work done this year leads to new questions next year, which then leads to further questions. The application of this scientific knowledge lags necessarily behind the research itself. An applied science like chiropractic or medicine should have as one of its goals the training of practitioners to have an interest in staying current with new developments and re-evaluating practice methods to include the new information.

It seems to me that this goal, currently addressed only by requiring continuing education for licensure, is imperative if we have any hope of correcting the misunderstanding about the chiropractic profession. Chiropractic must be better understood in order for it to take it's place in the world of health care.

Health professions, of course, do not exist in a vacuum. The entire health system must be willing to re-evaluate and learn about and from one another for progress to be made. The hierarchy described in this book as actually impeded this progress. Providers and patients should be thankful that the old system is beginning to break down, allowing an opportunity for all to rethink how the health care system should be run.

# 3

# How Do Chiropractors View Health?

Chiropractors have largely been thought to be the most radical, anti-establishment rebels in the health care field. The common perception is that chiropractors are against everything that medical doctors support, and for everything that medical doctors are against. Because of this perception, the public is wary of a profession they think is the antithesis of traditional medicine which has served them throughout their lives. This chapter is written to answer common misconceptions about how chiropractors view health.

It is thought by the public that you must either "believe" in chiropractic or not "believe." The premise is that chiropractic and traditional allopathic medicine cannot co-exist. It is thought that chiropractic medicine is a type of faith healing; that benefit is reserved for "believers." Further, some think that chiropractors practice a form of quasi-religion rather than a science, and that God is somehow involved in the interaction which takes place between the chiropractor and the patient. Recently, *Time* magazine grouped chiropractic with new age religions and quasi-scientific self healing movements.

Chiropractic was founded in the era which gave medicine the "germ theory" of disease, when infections were the leading cause of death in this country. It was thought at that time that chiropractors were anti-germ theory, and that perception persists today.

Because the chiropractic profession was founded is the largest non-drug, non-surgery healing profession in the world, there is a perception that chiropractors are "against" all prescription drugs and surgery.

Many people think that the chiropractic adjustment is the only health service chiropractors perform. Because of this perception, the public thinks that chiropractors claim the adjustment can "cure" any health problem.

It is thought that chiropractors are against medical research and scientific methods of investigation. The public often thinks that chiropractors practice the same way they practiced fifty years ago. Chiropractic is thought to be a profession that "works" without any explanation.

The public thinks that chiropractors are scornful of high-technology medicine, preferring to diagnose and treat patients in a "homey," non-clinical atmosphere with their hands only. Chiropractic is thought by some to be a "blue collar" health care profession.

It is thought that chiropractors are not interested in competitive professional education. Chiropractic educational institutions are thought to be second rate, low budget proprietary schools with only previous graduates as faculty. Chiropractic students are perceived to be rejects from medical colleges.

It is thought that chiropractors are against insurance companies and organized health plans, preferring instead to provide bargain basement, cash-only health care. It is thought that chiropractic services should be less expensive than medical services.

Allow me to finally put these misconceptions to rest by telling you what it is that chiropractors think about these subjects. The remarks which follow are representative of the mainstream of the chiropractic profession, and represent what chiropractic students are taught in the accredited chiropractic colleges in the United States.

## Are chiropractors against traditional medical care and medical doctors?

Chiropractors have been forced for years to be on the defensive from an attack by organized medicine. Many reasons have been suggested for this enmity;  among them economics, arrogance, paternalism and ignorance. These reasons certainly could explain the decades-long attempt by political medicine to wipe out the chiropractic profession.  This anti-chiropractic campaign is not a dream on the part of a paranoid chiropractor or two. It has been documented in a lengthy celebrated court case (*Wilk et al. v. AMA et al.*) brought by chiropractors against the American Medical Association and other professional organizations.  The suit claimed that the AMA had acted unlawfully by violating antitrust laws in conspiring with other professional societies to eliminate the chiropractic profession in the United States.  After a fourteen year court battle, the chiropractors prevailed and the District Court Judge who heard the case issued a Permanent Injunction Order against the AMA to prevent the continuance of these practices.

Putting the court case aside, what does the average chiropractor in practice think about medical doctors?  Most chiropractors are quick to recognize medical doctors as necessary members of each patient's health care team.  No chiropractor that I know wants to manage a heart attack, cast a fracture, treat cancer, or prescribe medications;  these procedures are considered beyond the scope of chiropractic practice.  There may have been a time when certain zealots in the profession would have attempted to treat all conditions with chiropractic methods.  To do so in the 1990s would be malpractice, simply because the chiropractic profession with burgeoning science has better defined its scope of practice.

It seems that an earlier generation of chiropractors may have had a legitimate bone to pick with the medical profession. Why? Before chiropractic was licensed in every state in the US, chiropractors were forced to practice without a license. Occasionally, the local medical society would conduct a witch hunt, and the chiropractor would be arrested for practicing medicine without a license. I cannot say how I would feel to have the sheriff handcuff me in front of my office or home and throw me in jail. I suspect that I might harbor a grudge, too.

Chiropractic health care is now licensed in every state in the union. The first licensing law was in Kansas in 1913, the last in Louisiana in 1973. Why the long time gap between the first and the last? Early on, political medicine got involved in chiropractic's attempt for professionalization, and because of the power and money associated with political medicine, they were successful in stalling the licensing in all states.

Even when these types of activities occurred with some frequency, individual medical doctors and chiropractors often worked together in harmony. These relationships were often conducted in secrecy because it was the official policy of the AMA that for a medical doctor to associate with a chiropractor was unethical. On a person to person basis, however, chiropractors who wanted to have a professional relationship with a medical doctor probably had one.

Early chiropractors did the profession a disservice when they failed to realize or admit the scope of their practice. When a condition clearly calls for a medical doctor, whether it be a family physician or a specialist, a modern chiropractor will refer that patient.

* * *

Winona was a middle aged overweight woman who had been coming to the office that I bought for chiropractic care for decades. Her previous records were often sketchy at best with regard to why she was being treated and her general health. As part of my introduction to each patient, I had all existing patients fill out new data forms as if they were new patients; I conducted an exam based on this information. Many of the existing patients were amazed and/or confused by my sudden need for information which the previous chiropractor had apparently thought unnecessary.

Winona appeared to be interested in my "new" methods. One of the first things all patients got was vital signs and weight. I screwed on the special blood pressure cuff which is made for heavy people and asked Winona what her blood pressure usually ran.

"I don't know, doc," she replied. "I guess the only doctor that I have been to for a long time is the chiropractor, and he never took my blood pressure."

The first time I took her blood pressure, it was 170/110. Too high. But not surprising considering her weight and lack of activity. I noted what I had heard, and made a notation to take it again on her next visit. After three readings, the average was 165/100. I was taught that this reading should be considered borderline, and a referral to a medical doctor was appropriate.

"I'm going to send you to your medical doctor, Winona," I explained. "Your blood pressure is on the high side, and I would like to get his opinion about treatment." I went on to explain that it is not uncommon to find these kinds of numbers in a patient who is overweight, and we talked some about her inability to lose weight, even though she claimed that she had been on every diet known to man. She agreed to take my referral slip to her medical doctor the next day.

A couple of days later, I got a letter in the mail from the medical doctor. He agreed that she was a borderline hypertensive, but indicated that he didn't feel that she was a candidate for medication. Rather, he suggested that we work together to encourage Winona to begin a walking program and make some dietary changes.

I was encouraged that this doctor and I were apparently going to be able to relate on a professional level. Over the years, we did just that, and I think the patients that we both saw benefitted from that relationship.

* * *

Modern chiropractors begin to form a referral network before they see their first patient. Chiropractors know that they will have to refer a patient occasionally to a medical doctor.

If chiropractic still has a bone to pick with the medical profession, it is that medical doctors don't show reciprocal concern for their patients by referring them to chiropractors. Many patients come to a chiropractor after a series of failed treatment with medical doctors. If the medical doctor had been willing to admit that he/she is not well educated in diagnosing or treating musculoskeletal conditions, the patient could have been spared a lot of time, money and suffering with a referral to a DC. Even the medical doctor with whom I had a professional relationship never sent me a patient. If a patient asked him about seeing me because they had failed to respond to medical treatment, he would tell them to go ahead if they thought it would help. But, as far as I know, he never suggested to a patient that they see me.

Surveys show that referrals to chiropractors from medical doctors is now on the rise. Finally.

* * *

Justin was a sixteen year old boy whose mother brought him to my office for neck pain and headaches. He had been involved in a rear-end auto accident six months before. Like many chiropractic patients, Justin had been through six months of medical care and physical therapy without a significant change in his condition.

After working through the history of the accident and symptoms, I told Justin's mother that I needed to see the x-rays that had been taken of him after the accident. One of the reasons this was important was so that I wouldn't have to expose him to repeat x-rays unnecessarily. She agreed to go to the medical clinic and pick them up for me, a practice which was common in my community.

The next day, she returned to my office and asked to see me. When I came into the room, she exploded into a narrative. "Dr. Brown won't let me bring the x-rays here because you are a chiropractor," she began. "I signed the x-ray release form at the desk and the nurse went to get the x-rays, but came back saying that she couldn't give them to me. So I asked to talk to Dr. Brown. While I was waiting in the hallway for him to come out, one of the other doctors came by and said, "It's too bad I didn't order those x-rays of Justin. I would let you have them.""

She paused to take a breath. I couldn't believe what I was hearing. I had worked satisfactorily with two of the medical doctors at the clinic, but had never had any dealings with Dr. Brown.

"When he came out, he just said that he didn't cooperate with chiropractors, so I couldn't have the x-rays. I know it's my right to have them, but I don't want to make a big stink about it. He might be on call someday when I need a doctor and I don't want to make him mad. Can you just take new x-rays of Justin?"

* * *

I'm proud to report that my son has always been extremely bright in school. The summer that I began practice, he was getting ready to enter the fifth grade. It so happened that one of the medical doctor's daughters was in his class in school. Not long after the school year started, Brandon began to tell us that Kelly, the daughter, and he had a competition going for the best grades. He had never been very competitive about grades, so my wife and I were surprised at his new interest in competing.

One day, he came home from school and said, "Kelly says that her dad is a medical doctor and you are a chiropractor. Then she said something like maybe she shouldn't talk to me." He didn't appear embarrassed or offended by what she had said. Puzzled would be a better word. I assured him that of course he could continue to talk to Kelly.

Inside, I was mortified. I thought I caught the implication, even if he didn't. What was even more disturbing was that Kelly's dad was one of the medical doctors at the clinic with whom I felt I had a good working relationship. I had referred a couple of patients to him and had spoken to him on the telephone. I had gotten x-rays, lab work results and daily notes from him on several patients. He had sent me follow-up letters on the patients I had sent to him.

I couldn't let myself believe that he had said something derogatory about chiropractic or me in front of his daughter. But she had obviously heard it somewhere. I tried to forget about the incident and he and Kelly went on being friends/rivals. I could not forget the feeling that I was helpless against even my son being involved in the medical-chiropractic controversy.

* * *

Recently, my wife was applying for positions as a medical transcriptionist, a position for which she has years of experience and is eminently qualified. She was interviewing for a position with a group of orthopedic surgeons.

One of the surgeons with whom she talked said, "I couldn't help but notice that your husband is a chiropractor. Does he practice?"

Thinking that he was just making polite conversation, she replied that I was a full time teacher and writer.

"Well, I don't have a problem with chiropractors," he replied. "In fact, I refer patients to chiropractors on occasion. But not all of the doctors in this office feel that way. Do you think that would make you feel uncomfortable?"

The implication that the wife of "one of them" wouldn't feel comfortable working for medical doctors was clear. The truth was probably that the medical doctors wouldn't feel comfortable around her. We wondered if the surgeons were afraid that she would go into the waiting room and try to proselytize surgical patients for chiropractic, or if she would try to tell the surgeons how to do their job. Why would the fact that *I* am a chiropractor make that work situation uncomfortable for my wife?

She didn't take the job and the surgeons lost their opportunity for a first-rate medical transcriptionist.

* * *


The orthopedic surgeon who had been recommended  to me by other chiropractors in the area was happy to see my patients, but then told one of them that chiropractic care was the equivalent of doing exercises and taking muscle relaxers.  This statement  showed the surgeon's ignorance about what it is that chiropractors do.

I clearly recall my telephone conversation with the wife of the patient to whom that statement had been made.  I had called to see how her husband was doing after I got a copy of the surgeon's dictated notes in the mail.

"Doc," she said.  "I wish Bill would come back to you for more treatment.  I think he was beginning to feel better when he asked you to refer him to that other doctor.  The surgeon told him that he didn't need to see you again if he would take his pills and do his exercises.  Since he doesn't do either, he isn't feeling one bit better."

I assured her that I would be happy to see Bill whenever he decided that he wanted to return to my office.  Then I erased the orthopedic surgeon's name out of my address book.  I couldn't refer my patients to a surgeon just because he was willing to take my patients.  I was going to have to find one who at least had the intellectual  or professional  curiosity to learn about chiropractic.  It was obvious that this one just didn't care.


* * *


I remember two patients who were nurses.  Both worked for family practitioners in group practices.  One told her bosses she was seeing me for headaches and was told, "If you think chiropractic is helping you, by all means continue it." The other wouldn't tell her doctors that she was seeing me. In fact, she didn't even want her car seen in my parking lot.

* * *

On a final note, it is interesting to note that many of the early chiropractic school graduates were medical doctors. Apparently, before political medicine got involved in their campaign to destroy the chiropractic profession, some holistic medical doctors thought that chiropractic treatment would be a good thing to have in their therapeutic bag of tricks. Eventually, political medicine was able to all but end this curiosity by declaring chiropractic an unscientific cult with whom medical doctors could not ethically associate. Today, many of our students in chiropractic schools have had some previous health career; pharmacists, nurses, and physical therapists are not uncommon chiropractic students. They have decided that conservative care and the autonomy which chiropractic has been able to maintain are good reasons for leaving their previous professions to become chiropractors.

## Must you "believe" in chiropractic in order to benefit from it?

This misconception is so common that I'll bet you have heard it no matter who you are. I recall the first few days in the community where I was going to practice, a town of two thousand people. As I responded to the stares of the residents (new people rarely move into small towns in Iowa) by introducing myself as the new chiropractor, many would say, "Oh, I believe wholeheartedly in chiropractic." So many people said that to me that I began to feel like a clergyman rather than a doctor. How many people respond to a new medical doctor by saying, "I believe in pharmacology?"

Chiropractic is a health science by any definition. As a science, a belief is not required. Belief implies faith in something in the absence of fact. Scientific research is the cornerstone of modern chiropractic. For those who are ignorant with regard to the science involved in chiropractic, I am sympathetic with your skepticism. I would probably not "believe" in chiropractic either. What I am not sympathetic with is a lack of professional curiosity on the part of health care providers which should lead them to investigate the current scientific literature before they make public statements about chiropractic.

The fact that much of the chiropractor's therapy is done with the doctors hands seems to bring a "faith healing" element to the perception of the profession. I don't exactly know why. Surgeons work with their hands, too, but I don't hear the same things said about them. In fact, people talk about a surgeon who is skilled with his hands, but I hardly ever hear the same thing said about a chiropractor. Why is this?

Modern chiropractic has sound explanation for what occurs physiologically when the chiropractor adjusts or manipulates the patient. The doctor uses feedback from the patient's joints to tell him how to proceed in the adjustment.

Doctors of chiropractic use a unique diagnostic procedure called motion palpation to diagnose joint problems in a patient. The basis of this difficult-to-learn diagnostic procedure is the function of the joints themselves. All joints in the body, like the large elbow joint, are composed of two or more bones which meet at a certain juncture. The purpose of a joint is to allow movement at the meeting place of these two or more bones. The patient's spine is composed of many small joints which are about the size of the little fingernail. The doctor of chiropractic uses the diagnostic procedure of motion palpation to test each joint. The science of biomechanics has determined what are the normal motions of each joint. For example, in the elbow, the movements are flexion (bringing the forearm up toward the upper arm), supination and pronation (turning your palm up and down), and extension (making your elbow straight). Just like the elbow, all of the joints of the body (including the spine) have these various normal motions.

Chiropractors have found that joints which do not move through these normal ranges of motion result in various health problems. In the spine, where all the nerves of the body exit from the spinal cord, these symptoms can range from pain and muscle spasm to distant problems like sciatic nerve pain in the back of the leg.

The information that the chiropractor ascertains from palpating or feeling the joints with his/her hands tells him/her which joints need to be adjusted. When the adjustment is made, the joint is encouraged to move in the range of motion which was found to be reduced and over a period of time, motion can be permanently improved or restored. When the joint motion is restored, the joint's relationship with the function of the muscles also normalizes.

This is what the adjustment is supposed to accomplish. It is in no way magical or mystical or has anything to do with faith. What does seem magical at times is the results of these manipulations. Because of this complicated relationship in the spine to nerves which supply the entire body, health symptoms which may seem to have nothing to do with the spine may improve after the adjustment. Scientists are not yet fully aware of all the mechanisms of action. However, patients with acute or longstanding problems sometimes respond very quickly and their improvement is often long lasting.

The notion that an element of belief must be present for any positive results to occur is simply not true.  The science of the manipulation is well documented.

The concept which probably gets chiropractors in the most hot water with those who think that chiropractic is a quasi-religion is the concept of innate intelligence.  While the idea is firmly entrenched in all medical literature, it is known as homeostasis, the ability and need for the body to restore itself to normalcy.

All medical science knows, for instance, that the human body has a carefully orchestrated response to bacterial infection.  The body is "intelligent" in that it knows to begin this response without any intervention from a health practitioner.  At times, the infection can become overwhelming;  then intervention is appropriate.  Many times, however, the disease is considered "self-limiting," that is, the body will be able to fight off the invasion and requires no outside intervention.

When a bone is fractured, your body knows through this "intelligence" to begin to heal.  Mechanisms for healing are set in motion without intervention.  A cast is applied to make sure that the fragments grow together straight.

Chiropractors are respectful of that "innate intelligence" or homeostatic mechanism.  Because we respect it, we are not quick to intervene, for certain problems, with medications or surgery.  Rather, chiropractors work with the patient's body using natural solutions to their health problem.  Chiropractors might employ nutritional therapies, conservative care and/or physical approaches to the problem.  If the condition does not respond to the conservative approach, then the patient is referred.

This conservative care model becomes problematic when the chiropractor is unaware of his/her limitations and fails to recognize signs and symptoms which require a more aggressive approach, viz. medications or surgery. If the homeostatic mechanism of the human were perfect and all-powerful, no health care of any kind would ever be needed. This is not the case, so caution must be exercised. Neither patient's nor chiropractor's wishful thinking or "belief" will change the course of health events.

### Do chiropractors recognize the germ theory of disease?

Chiropractors recognize that viral and bacterial infections are the cause of a great deal of illness in humans. In the last century, medicine has made great strides in treatment of infectious disease; first with the introduction of sulfa drugs, and then the widespread availability of antibiotics.

Early chiropractors may have questioned the germ theory right along with many medical doctors who were wary. When it was first postulated that "germs" which no one could see were the cause of much disease, the entire scientific community was skeptical.

More recently, new infectious diseases like Legionnaires disease, toxic shock syndrome, and AIDS have challenged the health community. The first order of business was to identify causative organisms for these disorders. Just a few years ago, the focus on AIDS related to the question of what causes it. The next question is how to treat these diseases. Along with cause and treatment questions, scientists must ascertain who is susceptible to the organism and why? Chiropractors have always been curious about this question. The last logical question in the sequence: how can the infection be prevented?

Imagine this scenario. One member in a family of four develops a cold. The other members of the family breathe the same air as the infected member, are in close contact with the cold victim, and may even be inadvertently sneezed or coughed upon.  Another family member also develops a cold, but the other two do not.  Why?  The answer is that two of the family members were not immunologically susceptible.  The chiropractic community is interested in ways to boost patient's immune systems to make them less susceptible.

How, then, do chiropractors treat infectious disorders?  Since chiropractors don't prescribe medication, many send patients directly to the medical doctor for care when they suspect an infection.  Other chiropractors identify with blood tests and physical signs whether the infection is viral or bacterial, and employ conservative methods to treat minor viral infections, against which antibiotics are useless.  Other chiropractors treat minor bacterial infections as well with nutritional advice and time.  Any chiropractor who feels that the infection is serious will refer the patient.  The decision for referral or treatment is a clinical judgement call.

* * *

A certain single parent family became very dear patients of mine.  The basis for their status as patients was the mother who had advanced degenerative joint disease and low back pain at forty due, to a large extent, to her weight.  One of her small daughters had headaches which lead to vomiting. Chiropractic manipulation had been helpful in both conditions.

I had seen this family once or twice when, on a Saturday morning, Sally called for an appointment for both girls.  When I came into the treatment room, Sally said, "I think they've both got the beginnings of ear infections. Can you check them?"

I looked in each little ear canal at mildly inflamed eardrums. The older girl with the headaches looked sick, her eyes glazed with a low grade fever.

I started into my instructions for mild infections; force fluids, a vitamin regimen, lots of rest, careful monitoring. I also planned to evaluate their cervical spine for accompanying joint dysfunction. The mother was paying close attention as I talked. At the end of the speech, I said, "If they're not any better by tomorrow morning or they're worse before then, call me and we'll see what the next step is. We may need to think about sending them to the medical doctor for treatment."

Sally looked surprised. "Oh," she said, "I'm taking them to the medical doctor right after I leave here. Whenever they get ear infections, I take them both to the chiropractor and the medical doctor. I used to just get antibiotics for them, but I found that if we came here too, they got better quicker. Now they only have ear infections about once or twice a year. Before, we used to have them about once every six weeks." She looked up at me, pleased with herself for having discovered this phenomenon.

I knew then of few studies linking a positive result for ear infections with chiropractic. More studies have been done since looking at immune system response to manipulation. I wasn't sure that treatment would help ear infections, but I was sure that it wouldn't hurt.

* * *

Chiropractors have been shown to be correct that long-term, broad-spectrum antibiotic use is harmful to a patient. Medical doctors have realized this same thing in the past few years.

Tim was a twenty-one year old chiropractic student of mine.  When I first saw him in the student clinic of the college, Tim was quite sick with an acute pharyngitis.  He had a low grade fever, lymphadenopathy (swollen lymph nodes), and was just feeling lousy. Not uncommon.  I sent him home from school and asked him to call me the next day.  He was worse, so I referred him to the medical doctor who accepted referrals from the college. He was treated with Ampicillin and was improved a few days later.

Tim then told me that he had been on Tetracycline (an antibiotic) for acne for eight years.  This therapy had apparently ruined his own natural immune system by not only changing the make up of his normal bacterial flora, but by not requiring Tim's immune system to function appropriately on its own.  I knew him for several years, and found that he was frequently plagued by staph and strep infections which he could not overcome without antibiotics.

The long term use of broad spectrum antibiotics fortunately is no longer prescribed with regularity for conditions like acne vulgaris. However, I am aware of a prescribing practice which continues to concern me. I teach with a physiologist who has an infant son with recurring otitis media (ear infections).  The child's pediatrician recently recommended a prophylactic low dose of antibiotics to be given all the time until the child gets a little older. Fortunately, my friend realized the risks involved and chose not to follow that advice.


## Are chiropractors against drugs and surgery?


The public often has the wrong idea about how chiropractors view health care in general.  The public thinks that we become chiropractors because we are "against" prescription drugs. Using the same logic, we would think that an internist is "against" surgery because he doesn't perform it or that our family doctor is "against" birth because he doesn't deliver babies! Podiatrists could be said to be "against" all other body parts except the foot, and optometrists would believe that all disease comes from the eye. When viewed carefully, these ideas seem ridiculous. Chiropractors are not against prescription drugs or surgery. Instead, we are against the injudicious use of these types of treatment. Many other health professionals join chiropractors in that concern.

* * *

I have heard of chiropractors who have taken their respect of homeostasis to an extreme. As I have said, I consider this a dangerous practice and would be leery of a chiropractor who says that there is no need for medications and surgery, ever.

The chiropractor who owned my practice before me was one who carried this idea too far. He felt that he was personally responsible to get all of his patients off of all medication. Patients told me stories about this chiropractor taking their bottles of medication to the office toilet and flushing them. He intimidated patients into not going to a medical doctor for all sorts of health problems.

* * *

This attitude, thankfully a minority one in the chiropractic profession, is, in my opinion, malpractice. Chiropractors are trained in pharmacology enough to recognize classes of medications, to be aware of why they are given, and to know about potential side effects. This training, while important for the patient, no more gives the chiropractor the right to remove patients from medication as it gives him the right to prescribe it.

* * *

Raymond had been a patient at the clinic I took over for many years. He had been a patient of the pill-flushing chiropractor, and I felt sure that he thought my predecessor's attitudes about medication were representative of the chiropractic profession.

Raymond, a farmer, was a man of few words. His wife, also a patient, was a sweet, talkative woman whom I was sure had railroaded him into my office. I had the feeling that he just couldn't be bothered to see a doctor of any type unless he was half dead. His neck had been bothering him.

The x-rays of his neck told the story. He had advanced degenerative joint disease, and I told him I thought we were in for a long haul before he felt significantly better.

One morning, after I had treated him for about a week, I entered the treatment room to find him smiling nervously at me. "I have to confess something to you, doc," he began. "I went over to the clinic yesterday to get some pain pills for this neck. I don't want you to think I would do anything behind your back, but you said this might take a while before it feels better, and I just couldn't stand the pain."

Before I could reply, he continued. "It's not that I don't have a lot of faith in you. I aim to keep working with you, I just needed some help with the pain." He looked at me expectantly, unsure of how I was going to react to this revelation.

"Raymond, I think you did the right thing if the pain is bothering you that much," I said. "You make sure and let me know how the arthritis is affecting your daily life."

Later, I reviewed his chart to see if I had missed a clue as to how much his neck was bothering him. He had told me that the pain "comes and goes" and that he would describe it as "mild." On subsequent visits, he reported that the pain was "already some better." I admired him for telling me what he had done, especially since he thought it would make me mad. It was helpful for me in communicating with him to realize the level of pain he had, even though he couldn't or wouldn't describe it to me initially.

* * *

I have known chiropractors who ignore symptoms in themselves because they refuse to believe that they might have a health problem which requires medication or surgery. A professor at the chiropractic college I attended dropped dead of a massive myocardial infarction because he refused to recognize symptoms which he clearly could have diagnosed in a patient. The doctor who started the practice that I eventually bought died of cardiovascular problems because he wouldn't see an MD.

These are isolated cases. Chiropractors don't prescribe drugs or do surgery because there are plenty of doctors (MDs and DOs) who do, and these doctors are readily accessible to patients. Chiropractors refer to these doctors routinely when the condition of the patient warrants the referral. Chiropractors and medical doctors are now regularly working together to treat patients both with medication and conservative chiropractic methods.

The decision regarding when to change from conservative care to medication is one that the patient cannot make alone.

* * *

I should mention one more topic under this question which is commonly asked by patients. That is the question of routine vaccinations for infants.

I have frankly been surprised to hear the recent criticism by medical doctors of this public health issue. I remember as a child standing in line at school for the oral Sabin vaccine for polio. I grew up in an era relatively free of communicable diseases like polio, mumps, whooping cough, and diphtheria. Media reports about bad reactions from vaccines didn't register in my consciousness until the swine flu vaccine fiasco in 1976. After that event, it seems, naysayers started speaking out from the medical community who gives these vaccinations.

I was surprised to learn, then, that chiropractic had a core of practitioners who had always spoken against vaccines. As vaccination became mandatory in order to register children in public schools, chiropractors began to devise ways to work around the system. One of the ways was to sign a medical exemption themselves if their state allows DCs to do this, or to find a sympathetic medical doctor who would sign the form. Another method was a religious objection to the vaccine. I have heard that chiropractors went so far as to develop a not-for-profit religious organization which would give their patients the ability to object based on religious beliefs.

I had a patient once ask me about this religious exemption. At that time, I didn't know what she was talking about. My son had been vaccinated before I even knew about any of the controversy. He had had no ill effects, but I couldn't argue with a parent who was well informed about the risk percentages. What I decided to do in my office was to have current information (pro and con) available to give to parents if they asked my opinion. It was my belief that this was the parent's decision and I shouldn't force the issue either way. In Iowa, chiropractors couldn't sign the exemption anyway, so the patient would have to argue with his or her medical doctor about the vaccination. I saw my role as a purveyor of information. Period. The thought of a group of chiropractors creating a religious objection is an abhorrent scheme which blurs the line between science and religion.

### Do chiropractors think the adjustment can "cure" all health problems?

It should first be said that while chiropractors' main therapy is the manipulation or adjustment, there are many other treatment procedure which chiropractors can and do perform. Many chiropractors use physiotherapy methods, such as heat, ice, electrical modalities, ultrasound, traction, supports and exercises in their treatment of musculoskeletal conditions. Many use nutritional and dietary advice as a large part of their practice, both to treat organic and musculoskeletal disorders. The therapeutic encounters with patients often include many types of treatment.

It is true that chiropractors have traditionally treated non-musculoskeletal conditions with manipulation. These conditions may seem to have nothing to do with the spine, and yet research with animals has shown that immobilized spinal joints can result in organic or visceral disorders. Recall some of my previous stories about patients who improved after spinal manipulation.

Second, the word "cure" usually sticks in the chiropractor's throat. Chiropractors have the philosophy that the patient's body "cures;" health care treatment is instead a facilitator.

* * *

Judy will always be one of my favorite patients.  She was a short, overweight woman with a chief complaint of low back pain.  She had been to other chiropractors over the years with some relief, as well as the local medical clinic, where she had been given muscle relaxers.  She was not satisfied with her long term improvement.  I don't now what brought her to my office.  As I palpated her to evaluate her low back pain, I found grossly dysfunctional joints at the area of her spine under her rib cage, known as the lumbar spine.  Her paraspinal muscles were in spasm on both sides.  Because of my previous patients with menstrual irregularities, I asked Judy if she suffered with that problem also.

She said that she had had painful menstruation and irregular cycles since she was a girl.  She hadn't mentioned these problems to me because there was no way for her to know that they might be related.

I began to treat Judy both for the low back pain and dysfunction as well as for the menstrual irregularities.  Her treatment plan consisted of spinal manipulation as indicated by the movement dysfunction of the joints, intersegmental traction (a machine which mobilized all the joints of her spine), and a nutritional supplement which I had found useful for menstrual irregularities.

Judy began to get some improvement in her low back pain.  Eventually, I was seeing her once every two weeks.  After about three months, her cycles had become more regular and less painful.

One day, as I was helping her onto the intersegmental traction table, Judy looked up at me and said, "You know, I feel better than I ever remember feeling.  What's more, I feel different inside."

What a boost to my day that comment was. The feeling that I had played an important role in a patient's quality of life was the reason that I had become a health care provider.


## Are chiropractors against medical research?


At one time during chiropractic professional development, anecdotal or empirical evidence was all that the profession had to use as authority. Patients returned to chiropractors in growing numbers because of the clinical results they obtained. Research was considered "medical" and was therefore viewed with skepticism. I don't think that chiropractors feared that research would show that chiropractic therapy was ineffective (it obviously was effective) as much as chiropractors feared that research would allow other health professionals (the medical doctors) to figure out what they were doing. If medical doctors started treating patients with chiropractic treatment, the fear was that it could put chiropractic out of business.

When chiropractic was first included in Medicare and Medicaid, some chiropractors fought the idea of reporting diagnostic codes and treatment procedures. An older chiropractor told me that the state association had concern that some "big brother" super computer would take all of this information and create a treatment protocol so that medical doctors could somehow figure out what we were doing with our patients and eliminate the chiropractic profession.

As I have discussed above, this idea was perhaps not as far-fetched then as it sounds now, given the tenor of the AMA's attack against chiropractic.

The chiropractic profession's opinion about research has changed. In the past two decades, chiropractic has made research one of its top professional priorities. Research departments are found at most of the chiropractic colleges. Funding from within the profession is growing. Chiropractic research projects have been funded by the National Institutes of Health.

In addition, chiropractors have joined medical doctors, doctors of osteopathy, basic scientists and public health experts in interdisciplinary societies, conferences, and research projects to further health care's knowledge and understanding of neuromusculoskeletal conditions. Research done by all health professionals is routinely taught at chiropractic colleges.

Another obstacle to research in the past was a feeling among some chiropractic leaders that research was superfluous and unnecessary. If chiropractic treatment worked, why should chiropractic concern itself to show why? This argument was hard to counter in a profession which was almost entirely represented by clinicians. As the profession began to give birth to writers and scientists from within, as well as to attract interested scientists from outside of chiropractic, the importance of research began to be better understood.

Chiropractors are beginning to understand that in order to take their rightful place in the health care community, they must be accountable to various other professional groups. Interaction with consumer advocate groups, attorneys, third party payers, and other health professionals requires chiropractors to provide answers regarding the how and why questions about chiropractic.


<u>Are chiropractors against high tech</u>

<u>diagnosis and treatment?</u>

There seems to be another misconception about chiropractic because much of the chiropractor's therapy is done with his hands. The misconception is that the chiropractic profession does not use scientific technology to diagnose or treat patients. Contrary to this belief, technology in diagnostic and treatment methods is very important to the practicing chiropractor.

In the diagnostic realm, chiropractors use thermography, muscle strength testing equipment, blood and urine testing, and other technological equipment to assess the patient. Advances in the technology of these diagnostic areas has exploded in the past few years.

Chiropractors have always made extensive use of radiologic imaging as another element in their diagnosis. Since just a few years after Roentgen's discovery of x-ray in 1895, chiropractors have used this technology to visualize the bones and joints of their patients. The last ten years have seen a virtual revolution in the diagnostic capabilities in this area, with first the widespread use of the CT scan, and then the MRI. Chiropractors routinely use these high tech diagnostic procedures to evaluate their patient's conditions.

While most chiropractic adjustments are still done with the doctor's skillfully trained hands, various instruments have also been developed with which to deliver an adjustive thrust. Other treatment modalities such as physiotherapy equipment and sophisticated rehabilitation equipment are greatly dependent on expanding technology.

Parenthetically, chiropractic doctors use computer technology both to increase the efficiency of their office procedures and in various patient education endeavors designed to teach patients about chiropractic science and wellness.

Chiropractors have historically been at the forefront in terms of diagnostic technology. B.J. Palmer, the son of the founder of the modern profession of chiropractic and long time president of Palmer College of

Chiropractic, was always at the cutting edge of diagnostic development.  By 1908, just thirteen years after the discovery of x-ray, Palmer was using the new discovery to help diagnose chiropractic patients at his school.  Over the next four decades, Palmer developed many instruments with which to diagnose chiropractic conditions.  The neurocalometer (1924) was an instrument which measured skin temperature on either side of the spine, a forerunner of modern thermography.  In 1935, BJ introduced the electroencephaloneuromentimpograph (!), an instrument used for reading brain waves and their conduction through the spinal cord.  This instrument was a prototype of the modern EEG.

Plain film radiology, still common in chiropractors' offices, was upgraded first with collimation and then rare earth screens to reduce the radiation exposure to the patient.  In the past decade, it has become increasingly common for chiropractors to use imaging centers to order CT scans, MRIs, and other specialized studies to better diagnose the patient's problem.

Some chiropractic offices use thermography, others employ muscle strength testing equipment to evaluate if the patient's problem has affected the symmetry and strength of muscle function.

The majority of chiropractors are concerned about giving the patient the best diagnostic service available, and have been quick to learn about new technology as it develops.

The chiropractic adjustment is still mainly done with the chiropractor's hands.  This combination of both "high tech" and "high touch" patient encounters is really a very desirable combination for the patients of chiropractors.  In the days of high tech, depersonalized health care in the US, this combination gives chiropractic patients the best of both worlds.

Should chiropractic health care be cheaper than "traditional" medical care?  While all providers need to be cognizant of rising costs, on a service for service comparison, I see no reason why chiropractors should be paid less than any other provider.

<u>Is chiropractic education similar
to medical education?</u>

It is not uncommon for me to hear from students stories about the ignorance which exists about chiropractic education.  A recent student told me about his best friend whose father is a medical doctor.  When my student announced that he was going to become a chiropractor, the medical doctor asked if the training consisted of a six-month course.  If other health professionals are as ignorant about chiropractic education as this man, it is not surprising that the general public is confused, too.

I guess you could say that I have spent a great deal of time considering chiropractic education.  I have been a student or a faculty member at three chiropractic colleges.  I am the author of a book on chiropractic education.  I am proud to be associated with the college where I currently manage the chiropractic division.  I consider this subject so important that I have devoted an entire chapter to it, but I will respond briefly to the question here.

Chiropractic colleges are fully accredited, not-for-profit educational institutions.  The specialized professional accrediting agency for chiropractic is the Council on Chiropractic Education (CCE).  Many of the chiropractic colleges are also accredited by the appropriate regional accrediting agency.  Some are authorized as such to grant other degrees as well as the Doctor of Chiropractic degree.  Several of the colleges may also grant the Bachelor of

Science degree, and two of them are additionally authorized to grant the Associate in Science and the Master of Science degrees.

The institutions are classified as professional schools. Students enter with a minimum of two years of undergraduate education, which is followed by four to five years of professional education. In this regard, chiropractic colleges are very similar to medical schools.

Unlike medical schools, the chiropractic professional internship is completed during the educational process at a college sponsored, ambulatory outpatient clinic. When chiropractors graduate, they are ready to take state licensing exams and begin to practice.

During the course of the education, all chiropractic students undergo a rigorous, three part National Board exam series. The successful completion of these National Boards is required in most states before an applicant can sit for the state board.

The curriculum at chiropractic colleges is, to a point, very similar to medical schools. Chiropractic students, of course, spend less time studying pharmacology and surgical methods, but significantly more time studying spinal manipulation, the neuromusculoskeletal system, nutrition, radiology, and physiotherapy methods.

Chiropractic students are not medical school rejects or medical doctor want-to-bes. I recently asked three hundred chiropractic students if they had applied to any other health professional school besides chiropractic college. Eighty-one percent said that they had not - chiropractic was their first choice.

### Are chiropractors against health insurance companies?

Over the past two decades, most health insurance plans, including Medicare and Medicaid, have included chiropractic health care in their coverage.  During this same time frame, more of the health care has been paid for by third party payers instead of by the health consumer himself.  As business increasingly pays for health services, it is not surprising that health care providers have begun to feel that they are losing control over their profession.  The insurance industry decides what they will and will not cover, and patients base their diagnostic and treatment choices on whether they are covered rather than on what services they need.

All health care providers are concerned about this phenomenon.  Chiropractors are no exception.  However, chiropractors have a shorter history of inclusion compared to medical doctors.  In the early decades of health insurance, only medical services and hospitalization were considered "necessary" health services.  Non-traditional, alternative, and elective services were generally not covered, or were covered only if an additional rider was purchased by the health consumer.  Because the patient began to expect his/her health care to be partially paid for, chiropractors, dentists, podiatrists, psychologists, optometrists and others began to lobby for inclusion in these programs.  Not only did inclusion mean that patients were more likely to use these providers, but health care inclusion became another step forward in the quest for professionalism.

Chiropractic was not included as a reimbursable service in the original Medicare and Medicaid bills.  In the early 1970s, leaders in the chiropractic profession began to work for inclusion.  In 1974, this was finally achieved, although strict limitations were applied.  The only reimbursable service in a chiropractic office was the chiropractic adjustment.  No diagnostic procedures would be paid for by the plans;  neither would any other therapeutic services be covered.  Further, the chiropractor must have on file a recent x-ray of the area they were treating, but Medicare/Medicaid  would not reimburse the patient for these x-rays. This limitations are still in force today.

State chiropractic associations began to lobby for what are called "insurance equality laws." These laws require an insurance company to pay all licensed health care providers in a similar manner, without discrimination. All health policies written in that state must then cover chiropractic services as they would medical services. Ninety percent of the states now have enacted such legislation. This legislation allows the patient free choice to choose their doctor, without threat of financial reprisal.

For many years, chiropractic health care was paid for directly by the patient. Chiropractors who practiced in those days say that it was a much simpler time to be in practice, and I'm sure that many medical doctors and dentists would agree. Those of us who were "born into" the current system simply view third party payers as part of the hassle of the current practice of health care.

The doctors who were practicing during the transitional time have had an extremely difficult time adapting to the increasingly bureaucratic regulations. Some chiropractors chose to disassociate themselves from the changing health reimbursement climate by first declaring that they would not file health insurance claims. As time went on, many became aware that they would have to catch up in order to maintain their practices, and began to work through the tangle of red tape to get their services paid for. A few others held steadfast in their decision to refuse play by the current rules.

* * *

While still in chiropractic colleges, my friend and I had invited ourselves to visit the office of a chiropractor who had spoken to our class. He was a little older than we were, a child of the turbulent sixties. When we arrived at his office, we were surprised to see a box on his reception counter with a sign explaining that he didn't file insurance, and didn't charge specific fees. The patient should put in the box what they could afford for the services he provided.

This seemed a little strange and unprofessional to Joe and I, but we figured he knew more than we did. I had heard horror stories about paperwork, rules, red tape, and denial of payment all through school. Maybe this was a good alternative.

The chiropractor took each of us in with him to see patients on an alternating basis. When Joe was in the treatment room, I sat in the reception area with the chiropractor's wife, who was also the office manager.

A new patient came out of the first treatment room. This was his first visit; he had been x-rayed and examined. He walked up to the desk to pay and make his next appointment. He opened his checkbook and asked what the charge was. The wife of the chiropractor pointed to the sign and handed him a brochure on the office policy of making health care affordable for all regardless of patients ability to pay.

The patient was perplexed. I could see that he had no idea in what amount to make the check. When he looked at the wife for some guidance, she said non-committally, "Write the check for what you think the service was worth."

This didn't help the patient at all. He had never been to a chiropractor before, and he had no idea what the service fee should be. I saw that he was trying to decide on a figure that would appear appropriate without being too small. He made out the check finally, stuck it into the box, and rather than making an appointment, said he would call.

The chiropractor's wife was smiling, apparently unaware of the turmoil the patient had gone through. I remember thinking that asking the patient to give a free-will offering was not the way I wanted to run my office.

* * *

Unlike the chiropractor in the story above, most chiropractors have attempted to conform to the existing reimbursement system. This does not necessarily mean that they agree with the trends they are seeing. Many of the leaders in the profession are working with legislators, lobbyists, other health providers, and public policy groups to try to shape the course of current events. The entire health care system in this country is in need of reform, and chiropractic leaders are anxious to have a part in shaping the changes. In the area of financing and accessibility, chiropractors are interested in assuring that their services are available and affordable to the patients who need them.

## Summary

I hope to have shown you in this chapter that chiropractors in general are not a bunch of misfits who can't fit into the warp and weave of society, or co-exist with the more traditional type of medical care.

On the other hand, I think chiropractors have had legitimate complaints about how they have been treated by traditional medicine. The recent court ruling against the AMA brings us into the daylight. From now on, health care decisions and policy should be based on efficacy of treatment, rather than on the initials of the practitioner involved.

This is the only way that the patient's needs can override the inequalities of tradition, ego, and arrogance that have surrounded health care policy for so long.

# 4

# <u>Chiropractors and the Popular Media</u>

Ask any average American thirty-five to fifty about a TV doctor, and they remember Marcus Welby, MD. Dr. Welby was an honest, altruistic, loveable human being who treated all of his patients with the kind of care that we all hope for in doctors. Dr. Welby also apparently provided his service free; finances were seldom discussed in his TV set office.

The over fifty population may mention Dr. Kildare or Dr. Ben Casey, both hospital based TV-doctor shows which pointed out the ethical and humanistic virtues of young, modern, technologically adept medical doctors.

If current sociological thinking about fictional TV characters as important role models is correct, these three fictional doctors and others are probably responsible for at least a part of the career decisions among those doctors practicing today.

When was the last time you recall watching a television program which had a chiropractor as its main character? If you think of one, let me know. I am not aware of any.

Turn on your TV again and scan daytime programming. Each of the network morning shows has a medical doctor as a health correspondent. Cable and syndicated shows regularly interview medical doctors for opinions on health issues. Even local stations regularly use medical doctors as "health correspondents" in the major markets. There are network radio call-in shows. Almost every daily newspaper has one of many syndicated health columns. Many magazines have health columns with letters answered by doctors. These doctors are considered "expert" even on health issues which are outside of their particular specializations.

When was the last time you saw a chiropractor as a regular health correspondent for a major network, a syndicated show, or even a local station?  Have you heard of a national radio show with a chiropractic host? Do you see syndicated health columns by chiropractors in your newspapers or magazines?

If you were asked to name a fictional doctor who gained fame as a character in a novel, who would you name?  Dr. Watson in the Sherlock Holmes books comes to mind.  Or Dr. Gideon Fell in the 1930s English novels by Carter Dixon.  Even English veterinarian James Herriott's semi-fictional accounts might come to mind.

Can you think of a fictional chiropractor who was a character in even *one* novel?

If I asked you to relate a television commercial which used an actor playing a doctor, or which uses doctors to endorse a product, what product do you think of?  Aspirin, acetaminophen, buffered aspirin, and ibuprofen have all used "doctors recommend" strategies to catch your attention.  Dentists are proclaimed to prefer one toothpaste over another.  Veterinarians recommend dog food.  The examples are endless.

Have you heard any commercials using chiropractors' recommendations for any health product?

Why is it that the chiropractic profession is not represented in the popular media?  What is it about the chiropractic profession which has escaped the public consciousness of this country?  Why are medical doctors, dentists and veterinarians considered representative  of health care in the media, and other professionals are not?  Why are the lives and activities of medical doctors interesting  subject matter  for fictional books, movies, and television shows, but chiropractors  are not?

It is well known that public opinion of professions can be both mirrored and shaped by the media.  When a profession like chiropractic is virtually absent from the media (except in investigative reporting), how does this affect public opinion of the profession?  What about the self-esteem of the professional?

The only segment of the media which seems to be paying attention  at all to chiropractic  is the area of investigative journalism.  Recently, there have been a number of stories and reports about the chiropractic profession.  Have you read what non-chiropractors  are writing about the profession in magazines like <u>Time</u>, or watching non-chiropractors  talk about the chiropractic profession on popular television shows like ABC's 20/20 and Good Morning America?

This recent media interest in the chiropractic profession seems to be a result of new major research  studies which have found chiropractic health care, specifically spinal manipulation,  to be an effective treatment  for low back pain.  Another reason for the recent coverage could be America's interest in alternative, conservative  health  methods.

On one level, the chiropractic profession welcomes the national media coverage.  Calling attention  to studies which have shown chiropractic to be an effective treatment  is gratifying for the chiropractic community.  It is especially gratifying when, for years, if the chiropractic profession was mentioned  at all, it was mentioned  with raised eyebrows and warnings to the public.

However, on another level the pieces seen recently which are written, produced, and presented by non-chiropractors have been, in many cases, factually incorrect. While they may not be grossly mistaken, these stories often miss the point of chiropractic health care completely, fail to discuss important issues, inappropriately edit comments, or talk to the wrong people. Many times, then, the stories reach conclusions which do not represent the mainstream view of the profession.

* * *

For example, in the recent 20/20 story, a chiropractor from the Boston area was interviewed. This chiropractor treated 165 patients on the day 20/20 visited her. While there are chiropractors who see this many patients, 165 patients per day is neither the national average or necessarily a desirable number. The national average for *weekly* office visits to a chiropractor is about 130. At 165 visits per day, even if the chiropractor worked a twelve hour day and was productive 100 percent of those twelve hours, the DC would be able to spend an average of four and one half minutes per patient. If the chiropractor took even an hour out of the day for lunch and such, the average time with each patient drops to four minutes. With many surveys showing that one of patients' number one concerns is being rushed through the doctor's office, many chiropractors don't see a four minute patient visit as a desirable goal.

The chiropractor in the 20/20 story said that chiropractors don't treat asthma. Maybe what she should have said was that *she* chooses not to treat asthma, but that many chiropractors do treat certain kinds of asthma with excellent clinical results. This comment was reiterated in the closing of the piece by Timothy Johnson. The inference is that the medical profession will be forced to accept the chiropractic profession on a limited basis *only* because of the recent research, which has all been on low back pain. Chiropractic care for any other condition, according to Johnson, is unacceptable. That chiropractors are good for minor uncomplicated back pain is all the medical profession is willing to admit.

The chiropractor on the 20/20 program, whose remarks I will bet were heavily edited, also remarked that chiropractors "desperately need medical doctors." I imagine what she went on to say is much the same as what I have written; that chiropractors recognize that certain patients will require a referral to a medical doctor. But the comment was abruptly edited implying that chiropractors feel that they are subservient to the medical profession.

* * *

How do you think chiropractors feel having their profession judged by others who, by their own statements, show that they know little or nothing about chiropractic?

A couple of years ago, I was back in my hometown visiting my dear great aunt who will be ninety-one this year. One of her great pleasures in life is to take my family to the local restaurant and introduce us to all her friends. "This is my nephew, Kent," she begins. "He is a chiropractor out of Dallas, Texas." This introduction is used to impress her friends on two levels: first, that I am a chiropractor, and second, that I come from so far away to eat at the Candlelight restaurant in DeWitt, Iowa with my aunt.

On this particular occasion, my aunt's friend said, "Oh, a chiropractor, huh? I just saw a segment on the health section of the news that MD's are now saying that it is okay to go to a chiropractor."

I smiled and the conversation moved on. My aunt's friend had brought up a subject about which chiropractors are very sensitive. On the one hand, this kind of report couldn't be considered anything but good for the chiropractic profession. Patients of chiropractors feel good that the two types of doctors seem to be getting along. But the chiropractors sometimes bristle at these reports. Chiropractors feel that these types of endorsements imply that the chiropractic profession is looking for the medical profession's permission or vote of confidence to carry out our careers. And since we know that most medical doctors know little about what we do, these types of reports seem even more meaningless. Have you ever seen a news report that says, "Chiropractors now say that it is safe to visit your medical doctor for certain conditions.

* * *

In the scanty fictional accounts of chiropractors over the past forty years, the chiropractic profession often commands less respect than a used car salesman.

In 1952, Burt Lancaster and Shirley Booth starred in a movie entitled, "Come Back, Little Sheba." Lancaster's character, a chiropractor, is portrayed as an alcoholic. Embittered and disappointed at his inability to become a medical doctor, he ruins his life by becoming a drunk.

This representation of a chiropractor who was actually a medical school reject typifies public attitude of decades past about chiropractors. However, for many chiropractic students, the chiropractic profession is their first choice.

A similar attitude was portrayed on a segment of the popular "Andy Griffith Show" in the early 1960s. Andy is pretending to be barber Floyd's son who is home visiting from school. Asked what he is studying, Andy replies, "Chiropractor." Floyd hold up Andy's hand and remarks that his big hands appear tailor made for chiropractic. The implication is that chiropractic is a profession suited to people with large hands; no regard for academic achievement is necessary.

In the 1980's, the situation comedy "Growing Pains" repeated the same stereotype. Dad Jason Seaver (Alan Thicke's character) is lecturing son Mike about taking school more seriously. He tells Mike that if he's not serious about school, he may end up being a chiropractor, hugging old men for a living. Chiropractors found this characterization particularly insensitive due to the fact that Thicke's real-life sister is a practicing chiropractor.

"Sophie's Choice," a 1982 Meryl Streep movie, also portrays chiropractic as a devalued profession which attracts sexual deviants as practitioners. Sophie (Streep) is accused of having sex with the chiropractor for whom she works. The profession is portrayed as one which invites perverts as practitioners.

"Doogie Howser, MD," a preposterous sit-com starring a teenaged prodigy doctor has the father character in one episode responding to his wife's recounting of a comment by a fellow cocktail party-goer by saying, "...for God's sake, he's a chiropractor."

"Seinfeld" did an episode in 1991 in which Jerry's friend, George, was complaining of back pain. Jerry suggested his chiropractor to help George. "Chiropractors don't *do* anything," was George's reply. Later in the show, Jerry does convince George to visit the chiropractor. When George finds out what the bill is, he balks at paying it. "He didn't *do* anything," George whines.

A "thirtysomething" episode included a woman chiropractor. Elliot succumbs to a blind date with Ellen's chiropractor who had helped her with a disc problem. The chiropractor is depicted as an eccentric, somewhat frumpy woman who can't make it through the date without adjusting Elliot (without any diagnostic workup.)

I find the comic use of chiropractors in the television and movie art of the day to be particularly interesting.  The Hollywood community, generally quite liberal in their views, have, for some reason continued to propagate the stereotype of a chiropractor as a charlatan, a loser in the health care community, or a sexual deviant.

This is surprising given the success of real-life chiropractors in southern California.  The Hollywood community has been among chiropractic's most outspoken patients.  At least one major studio, Columbia Pictures, in the early 1950s, had a chiropractor on staff as part of its medical services for stars, extras, dancers, writers, producers and musicians.  During the time that these people were benefitting from chiropractic care, not one positive story line about a chiropractor was developed for movies or television.

The lack of balance in the portrayal of the chiropractic profession by the popular media leads to a lack of respect for the profession by the public. All professional groups have been targets over the years for stereotypical comedy roles, but without positive roles to offset the comedy ones chiropractic's image suffers.

* * *

Professionals are often used for product endorsements because of the air of integrity that they lend to the product.  Think of products advertised on television or radio which proclaim "Veterinarian tested..." or "Nine out of ten medical doctors..." or "Dentists choose..." When was the last time that you heard a product endorsed by a chiropractor?  I know of only three products which have used a professional endorsement from chiropractic.  One is the King Koil mattress.  "King Koil Sleep Systems are designed with the assistance of and endorsed by the International Chiropractors Association for a comfortable night's sleep," reads the ad. Springwall manufactures a mattress called the "Springwall Chiropractic Extra Firm." Another product is Therapeutic Mineral Ice, a topical heat product. "Thousands of chiropractors now recommend Therapeutic Mineral Ice for their patients who need it." Short, sweet and very professional. These endorsements are like music to the ears of chiropractors who are used to only hearing their profession maligned or ridiculed when it is mentioned infrequently in the media.

* * *

Advertising by health care professionals used to be one of the issues which clearly separated chiropractors from medical doctors. The AMA ethical code forbade medical doctors from advertising in no uncertain terms for the past one hundred and fifty years. In the early 1980s, the US Supreme Court heard a restraint of trade case which had been brought against the AMA, and ruled that the AMA could no longer force it's members to refrain from advertising. (It begins to look like the only way the AMA will make changes is by court order, doesn't it?) Previous to this change, the AMA frequently pointed the finger at chiropractors to show that they should not be considered professionals because they advertised. Presumably, advertising was "beneath" the medical profession.

In the major TV markets where I have lived, I would say that now medical advertising greatly outnumbers chiropractic advertising. Attorneys (who's ethical code also used to forbid advertising) probably run a close second behind the MDs. All major hospitals now have an active marketing department. The chiropractic profession is no longer the only profession which advertises.

A medical clinic in Dallas brazenly and tastelessly advertised for personal injury cases coupled that advertising with digs at the chiropractic profession. Two women are in a kitchen talking. One says, "...afterI was hurt in that car accident, I was going to go to a chiropractor. Then I remembered that chiropractors can't prescribe drugs BY LAW." Voiceover. "At the X Clinic, we're medical doctors, NOT chiropractors."

In comparison to this tasteless and repugnant commercial, the TV advertising that I have seen chiropractors do is quite professional. These ads are usually designed to inform the public about what chiropractic health care is all about, as well as to advertise a certain office.

Chiropractor's print and yellow pages ads are sometimes quite another story. I have seen my share of embarrassing, out-dated, and out and out untruthful print ads representing the chiropractic profession. All chiropractic state boards have statutes regarding advertising. It is the responsibility of individual members of the profession to file a complaint against these tasteless or deceiving ads.

* * *

I am concerned about the passivity of the chiropractic profession with regard to the media. If the profession continues to let others (especially the medical profession) define chiropractic for the public, it seems doomed to be perpetually on the defensive. The public should hear about the chiropractic profession from chiropractors, who can explain what they do and why. The chiropractic profession needs to encourage and develop writers and broadcasters from among its members and grateful patients to man microphones in radio studios, to write columns for newspapers and magazines, even to write TV and movie scripts which include positive chiropractic roles.

* * *

I have always had the pleasure of working with first year chiropractic students, who I have found to be interested, fresh, and excited about their chosen profession. After one discussion in class about the public perception of the chiropractic profession and the need for individual members to become proactive, a bright young man came up to the podium.

"Dr. Boyer," he said, "is that really how the public sees chiropractors? Are they really that confused about what we do?"

I told him that that was my impression. We had already discussed how we might individually participate to change over time the public's misperceptions. I have always tried to be honest with my students, no matter what the issue.

"Well," he replied, "I'm not so sure that I want to be a member of a profession which is so misunderstood and devalued in society. I expected that I would be respected as a doctor, no matter what the initials behind my name."

I know how he feels. The commitment to become a DC is great, and the profession has helped a lot of people. But there is much to be done, particularly in the area of media exposure.

"Todd," I told him, "I understand your concern. Now is the time to think carefully whether you are willing to continually be a spokesman for the profession. If you are willing, you can benefit chiropractic. What the profession needs is people like you who have a strong feeling about informing the public."

I am happy to say that Todd decided to stay in chiropractic and will soon be an excellent DC. Other students who have expressed similar concerns have, after a lot of thought, decided to transfer to other professional schools. Recently, students with whom I have had this conversation have chosen osteopathy, medicine, physical therapy, and environmental health as careers.

As a profession, chiropractic would like to keep all of the bright, young students who have considered chiropractic as a career. But as a human being, I am sensitive to an informed, mature choice which fits the individual well. Chiropractic is not for everyone.

# 5

# The Evolution of Chiropractic Theory

Many of the perception problems faced by the contemporary profession of chiropractic stem from the variety of theoretical explanations which have been offered over the years for the success of the treatment. However, chiropractic's interest in looking at the patient as a whole and respectfully treating the patient as a person rather than a disease has always been recognized as a positive aspect of the profession.

Without question, chiropractors were forerunners of the contemporary holistic health movement. Even today, when there is still dissension in the chiropractic ranks over the emphasis of biomechanics and the role of the chiropractor (broad or narrow scope of practice), chiropractors do agree on the importance of treating the whole person. This holistic approach to the patient is no longer uniquely chiropractic. In fact, most health professions are now talking about addressing issues with the patient other than chief complaint. Emotional and even spiritual needs have been given more importance. Chiropractors have been trained in this approach for decades.

Chiropractors have always been proud of their interest in locating and correcting "the cause" of a patient's discomfort rather than masking symptoms, which is presumably the role of pain medications, sleep medications, and any of the many "anti-" medications.   Anti-depressants, anti-histamines, anti-biotics, anti-inflammatory  and anti-muscle spasm medications  all prevent certain physiologic events from taking place.  The chiropractor  is intuitively interested  in why the pathophysiology  is taking place in the first place.  If an area  is inflamed,  why is it inflamed?   If a muscle is in spasm,  why is it in spasm?  Chiropractic proponents  would say that this search for the cause is one of the reasons that many patients respond  favorably to chiropractic  care after these medications  have either failed or offered only temporary  relief.

The chiropractor  also considers the patient's lifestyle issues with more interest  than  many other  medical personnel.   If the patient  is repeatedly injuring his back at work, for instance, what can be done about this?  Perhaps the patient has a postural or congenital  defect which prevents him from being able to perform  this job without injuring himself.  The chiropractor  could pick this fact up on a pre-employment  physical.  Perhaps the employee is doing some part of his job improperly  and could be better  taught how to perform. Spinal health classes, which are extremely popular in industry these days, have been  going  on informally in chiropractors'  offices for years.  Maybe the employee is doing something  recreationally  which is setting  him  up for an injury on the job.  Rather  than just treat the patient  whenever he presents with this injury, the chiropractor  usually works with the patient to prevent, if possible, the injury or illness from recurring.

Patients  with chronic problems  may also have concurrent  lifestyle problems which can be either cause of or result of the physical problem  from which they suffer.  Patients with chronic headaches  may be having difficulty coping  with  the  stress of a job  or marriage.   Children  with  chronic musculoskeletal  problems  may be having trouble dealing  with stresses  at school  or home.   Persons  who are overweight  or sedentary  or weekend athletes  may have resultant  physical problems.  Recognition  of the problem by the chiropractor may be the first step in treating it. The chiropractor works with the patient if the nature of the problem is within his/her area of expertise or refers the patient if it is not.

The philosophy of treating the entire patient rather than just the patient's neck or back has its roots in ancient Greece with a physician named Hippocrates. Hippocrates was interested primarily in cause rather than symptoms; in recognizing the patient as a whole human being and not just a headache or low back pain. As modern medicine developed, however, doctor's diagnostic emphasis shifted from talking and listening to the patient to high technology testing and treatment without regard for the patient as a whole. Traditional medicine developed an interventionist approach; if the tonsils are chronically inflamed, cut them out.

Some territorial chiropractors cry "foul" when they read and hear medical doctors writing and talking about the whole patient. Most chiropractors, however, are happy for their patients that the holistic approach to human ailments seems to be fast becoming the norm in all doctor-patient encounters.

* * *

Chiropractic practices have long focussed on wellness health care or preventative health care. In these days of third party payers' dominance of the country's health policy, wellness care is still devalued and often non-reimbursable. Most insurance companies will not pay for physicals, wellness counseling, well-baby check-ups or preventative care. Chiropractors have practiced well-person health care for decades.

Walk into a chiropractic doctor's waiting room and you will find that a certain percentage of the patients are there for check-ups. Chiropractic health care is at it's best as a preventative service. Because chiropractors deal largely with chronic disorders, the idea is to maintain spinal health before the degeneration of these chronic disorders becomes irreversible.

This philosophy has traditionally been foreign to the medical model. Patients do not typically go to the medical doctor until something is wrong with them. As soon as the symptoms of a health problem abate, visits to the doctor stop. Chiropractic has always fought against this system. Chiropractors across the country have tried to encourage patients to think about health in a positive, proactive way, equating the doctor's office with preventing poor health rather than fixing it. This has been a difficult idea to "sell" to our culture.

* * *

Because I bought a practice which had existed for forty years, I "inherited" as patients a group of people who had used chiropractic health services for prevention and maintenance. One such family was the Smith family. Mr. and Mrs. Smith had two children; Dawn was in her early twenties and lived across the state. Her brother, Dave, was a college student who lived at home.

Without any encouragement from me, the Smiths decided to continue their monthly maintenance visits, as they had done for the previous twenty-odd years. I checked their blood pressure, treated minor disorders conservatively, and adjusted them when joint dysfunction was present. Dawn planned her visits to her family's home on the weekend of the visit to the chiropractor whenever possible. Occasionally, I wondered silently if it was necessary for the Smiths to visit me every month. I knew of only one study which looked at children who were raised under chiropractic care, which showed a positive outcome with regard to the frequency of common childhood illnesses.

One day, Mrs. Smith brought up the subject of their preventative care. She had been telling her new neighbor about me and the neighbor had wondered why they would visit a doctor when they had no health complaints.

"I told her that we had found it was cheaper to come here once a month to stay healthy than it was to go to the doctor after we had something wrong," she explained. "Dawn and Dave never missed school, and were much healthier than the other kids they ran around with. We attribute that, in part, to coming to the chiropractor every month."

I was pleased that the Smiths felt so strongly about the health maintenance care they had received from the chiropractor. They had made a choice which they felt had paid off for them.

A couple of weeks after this visit, we got a call from John, the dad. He had hurt his back lifting a piece of heavy equipment on the farm. He was coming in.

This was the first time that I had seen one of the family other than for their monthly visits. John was in trouble and he felt that he knew where to come.

After re-evaluating this new injury, I laid out for John the treatment plan which seemed most reasonable to treat his back. As I did with every patient, I tried to give him an idea of how long it would be before he felt "back to normal." He didn't flinch. His attitude was "let's get to work on it."

To my great surprise, John recovered in about half the time that I had expected. Within a very few visits, he was back to normal, and back on his monthly visit schedule. The maintenance visits appeared to have contributed to his quick recovery.

Chiropractic researchers are now beginning to ask questions about health maintenance care. Studies of this kind will follow patients for a time and look at their incidence of disease as well as recovery time. Researchers have begun to document the body's response at a cellular level to chiropractic care, and now it's time to step back and look at the response of the entire organism.

* * *

D.D. Palmer, the founder of chiropractic, wrote only one volume about the profession he had developed from the ages old health interest in spinal manipulation. The book, The Chiropractor's Adjuster, was Palmer's major contribution to the literature of the day. In the book, D.D. envisions the chiropractic doctor as a primary care practitioner, a model that the profession is still projecting today. "A chiropractor should be able to care for any condition which may arise in the families under his care, the same as a physician," reads a passage from his book. The problem with his assertion was that he proposed one therapy for every health problem possible - that therapy was the chiropractic adjustment. Palmer based this assertion on the assumption that the "nerve impingement" that he theorized was the cause of all disease. In this sense, the profession that Palmer was building was completely foreign to traditional medicine in it's explanation of health which had long recognized multiple causes for ill health. Palmer saw chiropractic as a complete alternative to traditional medicine.

Palmer's son, B.J., carried this "one cause - one cure" theory to an extreme. In order to be heard in his quest for universal acceptance of the chiropractic theory that subluxation of the spine causes all disease, B.J. Palmer preached the chiropractic theory (which he had elevated to a truth) with religious zeal.  B.J. was quoted in a speech as having said that for $250 and 12 months (the total tuition and length of the educational program at the time), one could possess the knowledge of all diseases.  He is quoted as saying, "Bacteriology was the greatest of all gigantic farces ever invented for ignorance and incompetency."  The Palmer School catalog of 1916 stated, "All cancers, tumors, asthma, appendicitis, deafness...have a common cause, namely - impinged nerves."

These statements, of course, caused an uproar in the scientific and medical community.  A medical doctor who had just listened to a speech B.J. delivered in Washington, DC wrote, "I at first decided that he was a common liar, but upon more mature deliberation I rather felt inclined to honor him with the more distinguished title of expert liar, but my conscience would not let me off so easy, for it was plain he was a damn liar."

This is the tone of the early relationships between the titular head of the chiropractic profession and the medical community.

Very early on, chiropractic dissenters of the often overstated claims and zealots broke away from the Palmer School and developed schools of chiropractic which were more academically oriented and conciliatory towards scientific theory.  In 1905, The American School of Chiropractic was formed in Cedar Rapids, Iowa with a goal to provide dissection in the study of anatomy, a subject B.J. was not interested in adding to the Palmer School curriculum.  The National School of Chiropractic, originally another splinter group from Palmer, was actually run by medical doctors after its move to Chicago in 1908.

Even today, each chiropractic college has its own personality.  To a much lesser degree than in the early years, a teaching emphasis on musculoskeletal problems versus a broader scope profession still elicits controversy today.

How could the idea that the adjustment was the appropriate treatment for every type of disease even been seriously discussed?  In 1895 when chiropractic was first developed, the science of neurology was in its infancy. Chiropractors knew that the health care of many ancient civilizations had included some form of manual manipulation.  They proposed that the adjustment of the vertebrae had a positive impact on the nervous system, which has been called the master system of the body.  Chiropractors knew that all nerves of the body exited the brain and spinal cord through openings in the vertebrae, called intervertebral foramen.  From these exiting nerves, all of the tissues of the body receive their nervous system supply.  Chiropractors called the interruption of the nervous system supply a "subluxation,"borrowing the term from medicine which means "a partial or incomplete dislocation." The theory was that "misaligned" vertebrae put pressure on the nerves.  Early chiropractic theory held that these "subluxations" could affect any system of the body, and result in any type of illness, from a backache to cancer.  The adjustment was thought to "realign" the vertebrae, thus relieving the pressure.

Early chiropractors treated any disorder, telling patients that if their nervous system was not functioning properly, the adjustment could restore function.  In fact, many of the patients who chose chiropractic treatment for a variety of illnesses did have health improvement, sometimes dramatic improvement.  The results that these patients felt after an adjustment often far exceeded the chiropractic profession's ability to explain how or why the improvement had taken place.  For this reason, the simplistic explanation persisted that the vertebrae had been "out of place", the nerve was "pinched", the chiropractor put the bone "back into place" and the pain or problem went away.  To make this explanation more understandable to the patient, nerve energy was equated to water coming out of a garden hose and the subluxation was said to be like someone putting their foot on the garden hose, clamping off the water supply. The chiropractor's job was to "take the foot off of the garden hose," and the nerve energy would flow again.

Because at the time, scientific knowledge of nerve transmission and effect was not well understood, this explanation perhaps made some sense. How else could science explain patients with both pain syndromes and organic disease who improved after an adjustment?

* * *

Some chiropractic schools expanded early on with regard to the therapeutic services they taught to students. While many taught only the adjustment, others taught electrical and heat therapies, nutrition and herbal therapies, and physical medicine modalities such as traction. These schools, National in Chicago for one, preceded the modern profession of physical therapy in their use of modalities to treat patients.

It didn't take long for the chiropractic profession to begin to lose credibility with scientists and other health professionals. The "garden hose model" and "one cause - one cure" theories were hopelessly outdated by the 1930s. Many chiropractors and chiropractic colleges, notably Palmer, stubbornly persisted in advocating this model. Further, the early idea that chiropractic subluxations were the cause of all disease deepened the alienation of the health community at large. Those in the chiropractic profession who did recognize that new explanations had been forthcoming were spurned by "traditional" chiropractors as frustrated medical doctors or "chiro-medics." The chasm which resulted in the profession can still be observed today, although the "one cause - one cure" reductionists are currently a very small minority in the profession.

Even though chiropractors were aware of the modernizations in the science of neurology and biomechanics, many chiropractors didn't change their explanation to patients.   In addition, some chiropractors who had been educated under this garden hose model were unaware of the advances in these sciences.   No effort was consistently made in the field to continually update the practitioner's conceptual model.   Many chiropractors still practicing today were educated under this old conceptual model.

Those who were educated at the "traditional" schools were extremely intolerant of other health professions.   Others were educated at chiropractic colleges which were very progressive in this area and encouraged interaction with other providers.

There was a great deal of diversity in how chiropractic was practiced. Those who were intolerant of other professions tried to treat everything. Referring a patient was considered tantamount to admitting defeat.   The "team player" type of DC had no trouble referring a patient, but seldom got referrals in return.

I suspect that all scientific professions see in their practitioners a difference in practice style based on when the individual was educated.   It is incumbent on the individual professional that he/she keeps up with the advances of the profession.  A scientific profession like chiropractic should be expected to grow in the application of its science.   Professionals must stay current.

In chiropractic, many older practitioners have spurned the idea of staying current. They want everything to stay the way it was. They are not interested in progress in research, new treatment methods, or interprovider relationships.   For them, chiropractic is an unchanging truth.   This mistaken belief actually impedes scientific progress.

Patients attitudes about what a chiropractor does, then, are formed by the chiropractor they use. If the chiropractor is one of the "old school" practitioners, he/she is probably still using an outdated model to explain spinal health to patients. You see, chiropractic's treatment methods have not changed much over the years, but our ability to explain what is happening has. A new practitioner and an older one might adjust a patient at the same joint and get the same result. The difference is that the new practitioner will talk to the patient about joints which are restricted in their range of motion and resulting soft tissue changes. The older practitioner will still be talking about a bone out of place. Science backs the joint motion model, not the bone out of place one. Terminology has also changed over the years. Older practitioners call their manual therapy adjustments. Newer practitioners use the scientific term manipulation as a synonym for adjustment.

So what's the big deal? Isn't this just semantics? On one level these differences are just semantics which is why the new chiropractor can still communicate with the older doctor. However, the new practitioner has been taught to translate terms so that the communication can occur. The new practitioner can also communicate with scientists and other types of doctors because they speak a common biomedical language. The older practitioner who has not kept up with the profession cannot so easily communicate with other professionals. Antiquated colloquialisms like "bone out of place" and "nerve energy" are not definable in modern medical terminology.

Beyond semantics, the explanation to the patient of what the chiropractor is trying to accomplish can be very different between older and newer chiropractors. The concepts of a "bone out of place" which needs to be pushed back into place (the archaic concept) and a joint unable to move smoothly throughout its range of motion (the new concept) are actually diametrically opposed. A typical patient might try not to move after an adjustment in order to avoid the "bone popping back out of place." Modern chiropractors know that a joint whose movement has just been restored with an adjustment should be encouraged to move. Joints are made to move, therefore immobilization is unwanted.

* * *

Maureen, a fortysomething farm wife had recently moved to my town from the northeast part of the state. She adored and respected the chiropractor whom she had left behind, and was obviously hoping that I could fill his shoes. Patients bond to their chiropractor in a way which is probably unique in the health professions. The major reason for this bond is probably in the "art" of the profession - much of the therapy is done with the doctor's hands, and that makes the treatment very individual and personal. I was aware from the beginning of my relationship with Maureen that I was trying to fill big shoes.

No matter what I did or how I explained what I felt about Maureen's condition, she seemed unsatisfied. She would sigh as if to say, "If that's the best you can do, I guess I'll have to live with it."

But she continued to call for appointments. I even sent her to another chiropractor, thinking that we just weren't "clicking," but after a few visits, she was back in my office.

Maureen acted like I had never treated low back pain before. No, actually she acted like no other human being had ever had low back pain before her. She had what I would describe as mild dysfunction. I couldn't tell her this, but *my* low back caused me much more discomfort than she was in.

One morning, after I had manipulated her low back and sent her home with ice and activity instructions, I heard her leave the office for her car. I was in my closet of a private office making the telephone recording for the lunch hour when I heard a treatment door open and close. Norene came back to my office and said Maureen was back. Or had actually never left the parking lot.

I entered the treatment room to find Maureen in tears. "I went to get into my car and the bone slipped out of place again!" she sniffled. Her statement carried the implication that I had somehow not given her her moneys worth.

Somehow, I knew that this was not the time to explain to Maureen that bones do not slip in and out of place willy-nilly. I had apparently not gotten through to her when I had previously explained the current model of chiropractic diagnosis and treatment. "The joints of your back become 'stuck,'" I had said. "They are supposed to move, and when they don't, you begin to feel pain and can develop other symptoms. The chiropractor encourages those joints to move with the adjustments, and over a period of time, hopes to restore full range of motion to the joint." What could be simpler?

I had failed to realize the depth of her "belief" that bones pop in and out of place, which had been perpetrated on her for years by her previous chiropractor.

What could I say to counter her long-standing, albeit erroneous, idea of what I was trying to accomplish with her?

* * *

Contrary to popular belief, there actually is much scientific research on which to base modern chiropractic. When naysayers proclaim that "we don't know why chiropractic works," they are only partially correct. Most medical professionals are simply unaware of the research which is in the literature regarding spinal joint dysfunctions. Unfortunately, many chiropractors are unaware of the research, too, particularly if they have been out of school for a number of years and have made little effort to stay current.

The osteopathic profession has been doing research in the United States for over sixty years. European medical doctors interested in spinal dysfunction have been doing research for at least thirty years. Scientists interested in biomechanics, a rather new health discipline, have contributed much in the past several decades. The chiropractic profession joined in the research effort in the 1970s. Most accredited chiropractic colleges have active research departments and use interdisciplinary research to teach the science of the movement of joints. As the research has developed in the area of joint dysfunction and its clinical implications, our understanding about chiropractic therapy has exploded. With this understanding has come new interest and respect from all segments of the health community. For this interest and respect to continue, the chiropractic profession must call attention to the research, both within its own members and outside the profession.

Much of the latest research focuses on the efficacy of chiropractic treatment for certain conditions. Patients are divided into matched groups. Each group receives a different kind of treatment. The results of the treatment are then collected with various outcome measurement instruments. In this way, the question of when chiropractic treatment is appropriate begins to be answered.

* * *

A study published in the prestigious British Medical Journal in 1990 has certainly resulted in much interest in chiropractic. This study, conducted over a period of three years, compared the results of low back pain treatment for 741 patients at eleven chiropractic offices and hospital outpatient clinics. Patients were followed over a two year period in order to evaluate long term effects of the treatment they had received.

The result was that "chiropractic treatment was more effective than hospital outpatient management, mainly for patients with chronic or severe low back pain." The author of the study, a British medical doctor, writes in his conclusion, "...for patients with low back pain in whom manipulation is not contraindicated, chiropractic almost certainly confers worthwhile, long term benefit in comparison with hospital outpatient management. The benefit is seen mainly in those with chronic or severe pain."

* * *

Another study, known as the Dutch trial, involved 256 patients with chronic neck and back pain. The patients were divided into four groups. The first group was given general medical advice (medication, bed rest, exercises), the same as a patient in the US might get from a family physician. The second group got physical therapy consisting of exercises, massage, and modalities. A third group of patients got spinal manipulation performed, in this case, by physiotherapists with three years of postgraduate education in manipulation. The fourth group got placebo modalities.

At both six and twelve months after the treatment, the manipulative therapy group showed far superior results which the investigators called "remarkable." It is perhaps also important to note that the group which received manipulation also had an average of less than one half the treatments that the physical therapy group received. Other studies have shown not only superior results with manipulation, but cost effectiveness as well.

These brief summaries of two recent studies are fairly typical of many research projects carried out during the past few years.


* * *


Chiropractic theory has been challenged by medical science from its very beginning. Chiropractors increasingly welcome the scientific challenge as they vie for a position in the traditional medical system. The importance of wellness and preventative health care, treating the whole patient, and looking for the cause of a health problem rather than merely masking the symptoms has been adopted by all health professionals. The appropriateness of chiropractic treatment is increasingly being shown by research studies.

Even when the theory was overstated and oversimplified, the chiropractic profession grew. Chiropractic patients received positive health results by the millions. It would serve us well to recognize that the chiropractic profession would certainly have died years ago had it failed to positively affect patients.

In fifty years, chiropractors will certainly have found new and more efficient ways to treat patients. The conservative natural approach that chiropractic pioneered will have become the patient's first line of inquiry in their quest for continuing health.

# 6

# Chiropractic Education

The story of the evolution of chiropractic education is a fascinating one. I am proud to be a part of the modern chiropractic educational process. Since the way in which a chiropractor was educated has a big impact on how he/she practices, what kinds of conditions he/she treats, and how he/she explains chiropractic to patients, a look back at the educational history of the profession should be enlightening.

Chiropractic education's history goes back to 1896, shortly after D.D. Palmer named his new profession. The pool of currently practicing chiropractors contains graduates from many schools, some of them closed but many of them still thriving. Since early chiropractic education required no more preparation than a high school diploma and the course was around eighteen months in length, there are probably chiropractors still practicing who were educated in the 1930s! It is no wonder, then, that the diversity of practice exists.

The improvement in the quality and substance of chiropractic colleges appears to have taken place on a slow and gradual incline. In many ways, this increase in quality mirrors changes in the education of all health professionals.

The educational upgrade in chiropractic was contemporaneous with societal advances for the profession.

### How long is the chiropractic professional curriculum?

The current professional curriculum ranges from four to five academic years, depending on which of the fourteen accredited colleges you look at. The programs are either nine or ten fifteen week trimesters (three terms per calendar year), or twelve to fourteen twelve week quarters (four terms per calendar year.) At the present time, no chiropractic college in the United States is on a semester system. Chiropractic students do not have summers off, so the completion of the program can be done in thirty-six to forty four-months without summer vacations. Many students study straight through the year in order to complete the program as quickly as possible. This is especially important to second career students.

Chiropractic colleges require between sixty and ninety undergraduate semester hours as a pre-requisite to matriculation. Most colleges recommend that the applicant earn a bachelor's degree before matriculating in chiropractic college. By the time that a student graduates, he or she has been in college for at least six years, more likely eight or nine.

This has not always been true of chiropractic education. The earliest school was in Davenport, Iowa and was run by the profession's founder, D.D. Palmer. The curriculum was probably less than three months, and many of the early graduates had previously been trained as medical doctors or osteopaths. Presumably, the early curriculum included coursework in the anatomy of the spine and adjusting techniques only.

Other chiropractic schools began to open just ten years after the Palmer School. By this time, the curriculum was generally six months long, and many of the schools had begun to include cadaver dissection and other basic science classes common to all health professional schools. Carver Chiropractic College in Oklahoma City, which no longer exists, raised the length of its program from six to nine months in 1908. By 1910, the year of the famous Flexner Report on the condition of medical schools in North America, Carver had again increased its curriculum, this time to eighteen months.

At the same time, the Palmer School had three diplomas available. In 1910, the student could earn the diploma "Chiropractor" after eight months of study, and could earn the "Doctor of Chiropractic" degree after twelve months. If the student maintained a ninety-five percent average in all coursework, the degree "Philosopher in Chiropractic" (PhC) would be awarded. The requirements for the PhC designation was later changed to include a post-graduate course and the writing of a short "dissertation."

Despite the diversity in the length of the curriculum, the first state licensing law, in Kansas, required a high school diploma and a one year course in chiropractic school.

By the early teens, the chiropractic profession had caught on enough that home study courses had begun to spring up. One of these was at the American College of Mechano-Therapy in Chicago. In 1916, an American University in Chicago offered a correspondence course in chiropractic. Chiropractic leaders were, of course, concerned about these correspondence schools popping up across the country. B.J. Palmer, in particular, was anxious to maintain control of the profession from the Fountainhead school in Davenport.

In the early 1920's, Palmer's curriculum ranged from twelve months for the Chiropractor diploma, sixteen to eighteen months for the Doctor of Chiropractic degree, and twenty four months plus "thesis" for the PhC. By

1927, Carver's curriculum was twenty months, while National was at eighteen months. Los Angeles Chiropractic College had an eighteen month day course, or a thirty-six month evening course.

National and Carver appear to have been the leaders in curriculum reform at this time. In 1928, National upgraded its curriculum to thirty-two months, Carver to thirty months. Both schools had added a full complement of basic science and diagnosis courses toward the goal of training competent general physicians whose specialty was chiropractic.

By 1935, there were thirty-seven chiropractic schools. The course length ranged from eighteen to thirty-six months of study. By this time, the profession had begun a move to upgrade the curricula of the colleges through uniform state laws requiring a certain number of total clock hours for the program.

The 1940s saw a movement for accreditation, even though the accrediting body was not yet recognized by the government. The National Chiropractic Association (NCA), later to become the ACA, was behind this movement. Most of these approved colleges were at or near a thirty-six month curriculum. Palmer School was not a part of this effort to homogenize and upgrade the education of the chiropractic student.

In 1953, the NCA Committee of Educational Standards recommended two years of college work as preparatory for matriculation into chiropractic college. Actual widespread implementation of this idea was ten to fifteen years away. Only three chiropractic colleges implemented the recommendation in 1953 despite the fact that by the next year, fourteen states already required the two undergraduate years for licensure.

1958 was the last year of the eighteen month curriculum at Palmer. For several years, Palmer had run two programs; an eighteen month program and a thirty two month program.

By 1961, twenty one states required the two years of pre-requisite education. Many also required a four thousand clock-hour professional curriculum. Most schools spread the four thousand hours over thirty-six months.

Finally, in 1973, the US government recognized the Council on Chiropractic Education (CCE), and chiropractic schools began to become accredited. When it became apparent that this accreditation was going to be very important in chiropractic education, schools that did not meet the two year pre-professional requirements either changed or folded. Palmer College, once the leader in chiropractic education, acquiesced, and in 1974 (twenty-one years after the first schools did this) began to require the pre-professional sixty hours.

In the 1980s, many colleges began to lengthen their professional program from twelve quarters to fourteen, or from nine trimesters to ten. This was the first lengthening of the professional program for decades. In 1991, Los Angeles Chiropractic College became the first chiropractic college to require ninety hours or three years of undergraduate work to enter chiropractic college (rather than the standard two years.)

The length of the curriculum is thought to have a positive effect on the quality of the graduates. With curricular time at a premium, administrators must be selective in the number of hours spent on each subject area. As the length of the program is increased, faculty members are able to delve deeper into certain subjects or add material to the curriculum. This presumably increases the minimum knowledge that the new graduate possesses.

An example of these curricular additions has recently taken place in the field of radiology. When I was in school, imaging methods like CT scans and MRI studies were not commonly being used by chiropractors. Today, these studies are routinely ordered by chiropractors and are readily accessible to them.  The need to teach students about these modalities is apparent.  The dilemma is how to include new subject matter in an already tightly-packed curriculum without taking hours away from other subjects.  As options continue to increase for chiropractic doctors, curricular time becomes increasingly precious.  Adding a term, then, has helped somewhat in relieving this problem.

What is the future of the length of the chiropractic educational process?  There is a move among educators toward requiring the bachelor's degree for matriculation, which is essentially what is required for most medical and osteopathic educational institutions.  In addition to the additional two years of age and maturity that chiropractic students would possess, requiring an undergraduate degree would even the standard for all health doctorate-granting institutions.

Many chiropractic colleges are looking at the benefits of moving to a semester curriculum with summers off for students to do preceptorships, benefit from remedial academic work, become involved in research, or just spend some "off"time to reflect on what they have learned.  Since most of the current programs include thirty hours per week of class time and sometimes ten courses at once, this rest time could be very important for assimilation of the curriculum.

## Who attends chiropractic college?

Chiropractic colleges have always enjoyed an interesting diversity of students.  The student body ranges from young students straight from college, second career students, and occasionally, retired students.  I have taught students ranging in age from nineteen to sixty-four.

This diversity of age makes chiropractic classes rather unique. Medical and osteopathic colleges are usually skewed toward the younger adult. Chiropractic has its roots in educating second career people; most of the Palmer School's first classes consisted of adults who had had other careers. Many chiropractic second career students come from previous health careers - nurses, physical therapists, and other types of doctors. Other second career students commonly found in chiropractic colleges have been accountants, engineers, teachers and counselors in their previous lives. Service to humanity and the autonomy of being one's own boss are common reasons for these students entering the chiropractic field.

I find that the older students often help the younger ones in the areas of maturity, stability, and responsibility. Often, the younger students help older peers with study skills, preparation, and college coping skills. This symbiotic relationship often makes the chiropractic classes like families. The competitive atmosphere one often hears about in medical schools is not as prevalent in chiropractic colleges.

Much of the competitive spirit found in medical schools is due to the extreme competition for the "right" residencies. Since the chiropractic student does his/her internship at the college clinic, the concern about residency location does not exist. Chiropractic licensing does not require a residency after graduation. Chiropractic students are eligible for licensing when they graduate from chiropractic school.

The chiropractic profession welcomes women students. About one third of the students currently in chiropractic colleges are women. This figure has been constant for the past several years. By contrast, medical schools have only recently achieved the twenty-five percentage mark for female students.

Patients are often surprised to enter a chiropractic office for the first time and find that the doctor is a woman. There is still a public perception that physical force is required for a chiropractor to be effective, and that is not true. While the practice of chiropractic is physically challenging, women of any size are able to become excellent chiropractors. This misconception also assumes that you have to be a large person to be a chiropractor. Instead, more important qualities for a chiropractor are the qualities which a patient would like to see in any doctor - compassion, empathy, truthfulness, intelligence, and virtue. In learning to do the manual therapy that chiropractors use, students learn balance, speed of delivery and how to use their bodies to the greatest advantage. These tools take the place of physical size.

* * *

My friend Carol, was a small woman of about fifty years of age. She practiced in a small farming community like mine, and I often wondered how the sometimes chauvinistic farmers reacted to a woman chiropractor. She told me this story to illustrate her winning attitude.

"When I first started in practice, patients would often come into my office for the first time expecting a male chiropractor. I remember one big, beefy farmer who came to see me. I walked into the treatment room and introduced myself as the doctor. 'How is a little woman like you going to adjust a big guy like me?' he laughed."

"'Oh, don't worry about that,' I said. 'I've never had a bit of trouble treating patients of any size. In fact, I'll tell you what, if I have any trouble giving you the best chiropractic adjustment you've ever had, the treatment is on me.'"

"The farmer laughed.  'You're on, little lady,' he replied."

"'I never had to give away my services,'" my friend laughs.


* * *


I have often been grateful when dealing with rather unsophisticated patients that I am a man.  It can be hard enough being a chiropractor in our society without the additional burden of having to convince patients that gender has nothing to do with the quality of care you give.

Chiropractic, like many other professions, is under-represented with minority students.  Many chiropractic colleges now have programs and administrators who are trying to correct this. Hopefully, minority students will begin to take advantage of special scholarships and grants newly available to them.  When the profession begins to look more like the world we live in, chiropractic services will be more accessible to the minority populations.


## What subjects are studied in chiropractic college?


Chiropractic colleges are much less parochial today than they were at one time.  The accrediting process, new to the chiropractic profession in the early 1970s, helped to homogenize the colleges.  The National Chiropractic Association's Committee on Educational Standards began the accreditation ball rolling in the late 1930s by establishing guidelines for the professional curricula at the nation's then approximately fifty chiropractic colleges.  These pioneer chiropractic educators developed criteria for voluntary, then unrecognized "accreditation."  Of the fifty colleges, only eleven responded to this call for an homogenous, upgraded professional program.

In 1973, the seed which had been planted by these early educators finally came to fruition when the United States Office of Education listed the Council on Chiropractic Education as a nationally recognized accrediting agency. With this recognition came new respect and opportunity within the chiropractic academic community. All of the chiropractic colleges operating at the time saw that it was important for them to become accredited. Some of the schools had never been interested before in becoming a part of the NCA movement. Minor and major changes had to be undertaken in some of these institutions in order to attain CCE standards.

Many people are surprised to learn that much of the chiropractic college curriculum closely resembles medical school curricula. Chiropractic colleges and medical colleges use many of the same books and study the same subjects with the same types of teachers.

Chiropractic students of today are taught in three general professional divisions. The basic science, or pre-clinical division is where the student is taught anatomy, physiology, pathology, biochemistry, embryology, histology, microbiology and public health. These courses are very similar to the basic science courses taught at any professional health doctorate school. Faculty for these courses are usually PhDs or holders of first professional degrees, like medical doctors or chiropractors.

Students spend the majority of the first two years in chiropractic college studying these basic science disciplines. At the end of the second year, students take Part One (of three) of the National Board of Chiropractic Examiners tests. This exam consists of six separate tests taken over a long weekend. The subjects tested during Part One are:

General Anatomy

Spinal Anatomy

Physiology

Chemistry

Pathology

Microbiology and Public Health

Integrated into the first two years of the professional program are the roots of the chiropractic science part of the curriculum. These courses begin to apply the basic science knowledge toward the goal of working with patients. Chiropractic courses found early in the curriculum include topographical anatomy and palpation, motion palpation (a uniquely chiropractic diagnostic skill), the history of the chiropractic profession, ethics, critical thinking, and the like. These courses are taught by chiropractors who have committed their careers to academic pursuits.

By the beginning of the third year of the academic program, most of the basic science courses are completed. The student then begins to learn general diagnosis, neuromusculoskeletal diagnosis, radiology, and chiropractic treatment procedures. These courses are taught by chiropractors or other clinicians.

* * *

During the time that I was in practice in Iowa, the chiropractic association lobbied for, and won the right to perform school physicals, high school athletic physicals, and Department of Transportation physicals for school bus drivers. Although chiropractors had been trained in physical diagnosis for years, the old regulations stated that only medical doctors or doctors of osteopathy could perform these physicals.

When I got the information to register as a physician who could perform these exams, I was startled to find that there was a section asking for transcripts of physical diagnosis classes. After a little investigation, I learned that physical diagnosis had not been taught at my chiropractic college until just a few years before I matriculated. Obviously and correctly, the state wanted to make sure that the chiropractor had actually been taught physical diagnosis.

This is yet another example of how the education of the chiropractor has changed very recently. Public knowledge of these changes in the profession are vital for understanding the role of the chiropractor.

* * *

In the third or fourth year of the curriculum, students study the associated clinical sciences of clinical nutrition, psychology, emergency procedures, obstetrics and gynecology, pharmacology, physiotherapy and other treatment regimens which prepare them to function as primary health practitioners. Students graduate with diagnostic and therapeutic skills equal to the task of working with patients.

The second part of the National Boards is taken during the senior year. This test consists of exams on the following subjects:

General Diagnosis

Neuromusculoskeletal Diagnosis

X-Ray

Principles of Chiropractic

Practice of Chiropractic

Associated Clinical Sciences

The student is now ready to enter the clinical part of the curriculum. Most schools have what is known as the Student Clinic, where the fledgling student doctor begins to treat other students, student families, and college staff under the watchful eye of licensed staff chiropractors.

When this portion of the clinic is completed, the student moves on to the college's Public Clinic, and begins to treat what are known as outpatients or "real" patients. They spend a year in this setting, again under the supervision of a licensed clinician. The student doctor is gradually allowed to assume more and more responsibility of the patient's care.

Before a chiropractor can be licensed in most states, he or she must take Part Three of the National Boards, which is also called the Written Clinical Competency Exam.

The state licensing procedure is completed in most states by sitting for an individual state exam which usually includes oral demonstrations of competency in diagnosis and chiropractic treatment, as well as radiology and knowledge of that state's scope of practice.

The subjects studied in the professional chiropractic curriculum, and the myriad of testing which occurs throughout the program are designed to produce a well-educated and competent Doctor of Chiropractic. The rationale behind the rigors of the program is that part of the educational institution's responsibility is to assure both the public and the profession itself that a competent "product" has been produced in every new graduate.

### How does chiropractic college differ from medical school?

Almost all medical schools require that applicants have earned a bachelor's degree prior to matriculation. A few have "early admission" programs which allow the student to study two or three years in an undergraduate institution, matriculate into medical school, and receive a bachelor's degree from the undergraduate institution after the second year of medical school.

Chiropractic colleges require either two or three years of undergraduate preparation before matriculation. The subjects required (biology, inorganic and organic chemistry, and physics) are the same for both chiropractic and medical schools. Some of the chiropractic colleges are also accredited by the regional accrediting agencies to award the bachelor's degree with a combination of undergraduate and chiropractic college credits. At this time, no chiropractic college requires the bachelor's degree to matriculate.

Medical schools have typically been very competitive with respect to admission. They have many more applicants than seats for each entering class. This fact forces medical schools to place much more emphasis on grade point average, interviews, and the standardized admission test (the MCAT) scores than chiropractic colleges.

Chiropractic colleges have traditionally been much more accessible than medical schools. The grade point average of chiropractic college matriculants is just below a "B" average. The result is that more applicants are accepted at chiropractic colleges than at medical schools.

The chiropractic profession has no standardized admission test like the MCAT. Instead, chiropractic colleges use grade point average, interviews and references to evaluate applicants.

The professional program in chiropractic colleges is four to five academic years in length. The medical program is four years in length, followed by a residency of varying length depending on the specialty selected. Chiropractic school graduates are ready to be licensed in most states as soon as they graduate. Their clinical internship is done at college clinics within the four to five year program.

The first two years of the chiropractic and medical programs are very similar. The same basic science courses are taught at both schools. After these first two years, chiropractic students begin to take courses on chiropractic diagnosis and treatment. Medical students often rotate through clerkships which expose them to various specialties within medicine. Chiropractic students have less curricular hours in pharmacology and surgery, but many more hours in neuromusculoskeletal diagnosis and treatment, radiology, physiotherapy, nutrition and biomechanics. The total number of curricular clock hours is very similar.

## What are the common misconceptions about chiropractic education?

We have already discussed many of the common misconceptions about chiropractic education. When I am asked about chiropractic colleges, I am most often asked about the length of the program, the types of students found in chiropractic colleges, what subjects are taught, and how chiropractic colleges compare to medical schools.

Decades ago, chiropractic colleges were proprietary schools. Since higher education in our country is primarily delivered by not-for-profit educational institutions, chiropractic colleges one by one dropped their proprietary status in favor of not-for-profit status. This was one of the earliest steps in professionalizing the colleges.

The G.I. Bill for returning World War II soldiers was very important for the chiropractic profession. For the first time, students received government assistance to attend chiropractic colleges. The next most important event was probably recognition of the Council on Chiropractic Education, allowing chiropractic students to receive federal and state financial aid programs. These programs, available only to accredited colleges, have done much to legitimize chiropractic education.

The chiropractic colleges have successfully overcome the "trade school" stigma of the earlier part of the century to become professional schools in every regard. All of the issues we have discussed have played a part in this scenario.

## What is in the future for chiropractic education?

Chiropractic colleges in the future will begin to require a bachelor's degree for entrance into the program. All other health doctorate schools already require this. The bachelor's degree will insure that the student is a little more mature, has shown that he/she can complete an academic program, and will help to insure that the graduating doctor of chiropractic is a peer educationally with other types of doctors.

Chiropractic college will eventually acquiesce, join the rest of academia, and move toward a semester program. This move has many advantages;  the rest of higher education is already on the semester system, students would be able to earn money in between years without jeopardizing their studies, those who require remedial work in a certain subject would be able to "catch up" with intensive summer sessions. Other students would be free to preceptor with practicing chiropractors to gain insight into the "real world." Faculty would have time to become more involved in research, writing, post-doctorate education, and other faculty development activities.

Chiropractic colleges will eventually cease to be free-standing, private educational institutions. They will begin to merge with universities and state higher education systems. Osteopathic schools have made this move in recent years with excellent results. The wealth that state university affiliation offers in the areas of faculty development, research opportunities, lower tuition, and professional recognition is self-evident. Interdisciplinary clinical opportunities for the faculty and students could begin to redefine health care.

Research activities at chiropractic colleges will continue to grow. The chiropractic profession is only recently beginning to realize it's potential in research as funding sources for this expensive task are tapped. Research activities are at the heart of the college's upgrading activities from trade schools to professional colleges.

* * *

Much change has occurred in the field of chiropractic education in the years since D.D. Palmer first began to teach students about spinal manipulation. From small, poorly equipped proprietary schools to the modern, fully accredited chiropractic colleges, the improvement effort continues. While chiropractic educators are proud of the schools in which they teach, all recognize the need to continue to improve the educational experience of the future of the profession. Obstacles like ignorance and prejudice about chiropractic are slowly being peeled away in the effort to help chiropractic health care reach its full potential.

# 7

# The Health System
# Hierarchy

It should be self-evident from the previous chapters that the traditional medical system has not welcomed chiropractic health care into the fold with open arms.

The chiropractic profession should not feel, however, that it has been singled out in this attitude of intolerance. Many other health professions have also dealt with this lack of acceptance; some have even faded into oblivion as a result of it. Homeopathy was effectively wiped out in the US soon after the Flexner Report in 1910, although it continues to flourish as a health system in other parts of the world. Naturopathy has been reduced to two small professional schools with only a handful of states continuing to license naturopaths. Health professions which have been tolerated by the medical profession (physician assistants, nurse practitioners, and physical therapists) have, as part of their professional roles, a built-in subservience to the medical doctor. Chiropractors have successfully resisted this subservience for almost a century.

Because of this resistance for autonomy, the chiropractic profession has had to fight against the giant AMA for every practice right it has obtained. These fights have resulted at times in a stalemate of cooperation which would have benefitted the patient.  In the past, chiropractors were sometimes unable to work with medical doctors for the good of the patient because of the restrictive medical code of ethics, which disallowed such cooperation.  Even today, when cooperation is sanctioned on the surface, more chiropractors still refer to medical doctors than the reverse. Medical doctors continue to appear threatened by referring to practitioners other than themselves.

There is, however, a growing awareness among the public about mutual respect of health practitioners, professional contribution and team work which appears to be positive.  The traditional medical system is being challenged from all corners:  patients, insurance companies, and practitioners themselves are beginning to question the time-honored system which is apparently not serving the health needs of the public as well as it should.  The health care system, which at one time was above reproach, is now being looked at under the microscope by politicians, business and industry, and consumer groups. All are calling for change.

The system which currently exists has been virtually unchallenged for decades.  It has become a hierarchy which shows signs of teetering as we enter the last decade of the twentieth century.  It is beyond the scope of this book to look at the economic and political issues surrounding health care, although these issues are certainly important and germane to the discussion. I am interested in describing to you the traditional roles within the system, and how these roles have affected the quality of patient care.

* * *

The health care system in the United States has for decades operated as a three-tiered pyramid.  At the pinnacle of the health careers is the venerable medical doctor, formerly unquestioned and untouchable by all other practitioners.  The medical doctor has an unlimited scope of practice.  The initials MD allow him to legally practice any health care procedure he wishes to practice, without regard to whether he has had appropriate training for that procedure.  Recent media attention regarding cosmetic surgery points out the problems associated with an unlimited scope of practice.  Board certified cosmetic surgeons warn the consumer public to make sure the MD they're visiting has been trained in plastic surgery.  This warning comes because it is possible for an MD to legally practice cosmetic surgery without any training in it.  Cosmetic surgery is only one example.  Since a medical license allows the doctor to perform any procedure he desires, it is up to the unwitting public to check credentials.  Medical care has become a "buyer beware" purchase.

A medical degree has traditionally granted absolute authority to it's holder regarding all of health care.  The medical doctor gives nutritional advice even though medical school curricula have little or no instruction in nutrition.  Medical doctors routinely give advice about the necessity (or perceived lack of it) for non-traditional services like chiropractic health care, even though they know little or nothing about chiropractic theory or practice.  I have often heard a medical doctor use fifty year old chiropractic theory to explain why patients should not use a chiropractor.  The current spokesman for the AMA is guilty of this.  Perhaps if he kept up with the scientific literature on chiropractic care, the topic could be more intelligently discussed.

Unfortunately, the public still tends to view the medical doctor as the final authority on health care.  It is the medical doctor who we have all trusted and believed in, whose word was sacred.  For equality, sensibility, and maximum benefit for the patient, this omniscient facade must begin to crumble.  Medical doctors are, of course, unwilling to have this "high priest of health" position taken from them.  Fear of this happening has pushed them to some rather shocking actions, as witnessed in the previously mentioned anti-trust case brought against the AMA by four chiropractors.


* * *


The second tier of the traditional pyramid has been reserved for health providers who work under the prescription of the medical doctor. This tier is composed of nurses, pharmacists, physical therapists, and physician assistants. It is at the medical doctor's request and instruction that they are able to provide their services. These well-educated providers are generally not allowed to initiate health services for a patient. Instead, they have to wait until the medical doctor tells the patient to go to one of these "second class" health providers for help.

Members of these professions have begun to rebel against the idea that the medical doctor is all-knowing. They have recently been somewhat successful in challenging medical doctors for more autonomous roles in patient care. In some states, physical therapists have fought for and earned the right to be primary providers. Pharmacists in some states may prescribe medications which were previously available only on prescription by a medical doctor. Nurses have begun to expand their roles by legislation and increased education.


* * *


On the third tier are the practitioners who continue to fight to treat patients without the approval or prescription of a medical doctor. These practitioners are the nurse midwife, chiropractor, psychologist, podiatrist, optometrist, and others. These practitioners have long stated that medical doctors are not the only qualified experts in health care, and have suffered from a lack of professional respect as a result of the adverse public opinion that medical doctors encouraged. Strangely, these practitioners have much more autonomy than the second tier, yet are often considered by the public as less legitimate. Perhaps this is true because the tier three professionals have disassociated themselves with the medical doctor. The tier two professionals, while subservient, are still associated with the traditional system.

* * *

Think about your upbringing. Where did your mother take you when you were sick? If you are typical, it was to the medical doctor, of course. Many of us didn't even realize that there were other types of doctors available. If for some reason you went to a chiropractor, you certainly wouldn't tell your medical doctor. The fear of his scathing reproach for not trusting in the majority system prevented such disclosure. A doctor of osteopathy was considered second-class to a medical doctor. However, many osteopaths practiced in areas where there was limited access to a medical doctor and they gradually became an acceptable alternative. If, however, you routinely used an "alternative" practitioner, you were equated with the client of a crystal ball reader or psychic.

The sentiment of the public toward alternative providers seemed to be, "If he or she is so good, why isn't he/she a medical doctor?" Sometimes this question arises just out of curiosity; sometimes out of ignorance; sometimes out of arrogance.

* * *

I was a retail manager at JCPenney before I returned to college to become a DC. Terry worked part time in security while he was attending chiropractic college. Terry was in my office one day telling me about what he was learning at school. "Why didn't you go to school to become a real doctor?" I asked innocently. I meant a medical doctor, of course.

Terry looked at me as if I had slapped him across the face. I knew immediately that I had said something wrong, but I still wasn't sure what it was. "Kent, chiropractors are "real" doctors. They're just trained to do different things than medical doctors. Dentists are doctors, so are veterinarians. Not medical doctors, but "real" doctors just the same."

I realized then that my question had seemed punitive. I apologized for my injudicious choice of words, which is all it was.

When the public is encouraged to see all health professionals as important, contributing members of the total health care team, this mistakenly narrow view of health authority begins to fade.

* * *

There is a pecking order even within the second tier of the hierarchy. My introduction to health careers came when I worked as a hospital nursing assistant in the late 1970s. Health careers and the education required for them had always fascinated me. It didn't take me long to figure out that a hierarchy existed within the nursing professions.

At the top of the nursing hierarchy are the nurse practitioners. These nurses have advanced education, sometimes master's degrees, and certification as specialists. A nurse practitioner is as close to being a medical doctor as you can be without actually being one. Considered equal, but functioning in a different capacity are the Certified Registered Nurse Anesthetists (CRNA).

These registered nurses have additional training which enable them to administer anesthesia. Nurse practitioners and CRNAs are able to make diagnoses and treatment decisions like any primary care provider, but must work in a "collegial" or "supervised" relationship with a physician.

Next, in descending order, are the Bachelor of Science Degree (BSN) registered nurses. (The designation of RN is a license, not a degree.) These nurses were less common in the 1970s than they are today, but even at that time the nursing profession journals were predicting that BSN nurses were the professional nurses of the future. BSN nurses have been educated in a four year curriculum, which includes liberal arts courses as well as nursing course work and clinical experience. The nursing profession encouraged the widespread commencement of BSN programs around the country as a step in its own professionalization. Their goal was to begin the upgrade to make the generic nursing degree a BSN rather than a two or three year diploma. The BSN is now almost universally considered the minimum requirement for supervisory and administrative nursing jobs, at least in major medical centers.

In 1977, the city in which I lived offered four different nursing programs. The newest program was the four year BSN program which had been opened on the campus of a small four year liberal arts college. The only other nursing program associated with a college was the Associate Degree in Nursing (ADN) program at the community college. ADN programs are two year programs which train the student to pass licensing boards to become an RN.

For decades, diploma schools associated with hospitals were the main type of educational institution in the nursing profession. My city had two of these schools. One was a three year diploma program. The other was a two year diploma program. The problem becomes self-evident when you realize that all of these nurses have the same license. An RN is an RN, whether she has attended a college for four years, a community college for two years, a hospital school for three years, or a hospital school for two years. The hospital schools claimed that they provided superior education over the community colleges, the three year diploma schools claimed obvious superiority over the two year schools, and the BSN program looked haughtily at all the others.

As if the RN situation doesn't create enough confusion, the term "nurse" is claimed by yet another group - the Licensed Professional Nurse (LPN). These nurses (Licensed *Vocational* Nurse (LVN) in some geographic locations) attend one year of school. Still a nurse, but limited in her function, a great deal of bad feelings existed between these two types of nurses. The LPN was not allowed to start intravenous solutions or administer intravenous medications. Presumably, this rule is not because these skills are so difficult to master; rather, so the LPN remembers her place in the hierarchy. On my floor, the LPN was not allowed to be a "charge nurse," and she was denied the pleasure (?) of making rounds with doctors.

Remember that no distinction is made administratively regarding who is the better nurse, the LPN is lower on the pecking order because of education only. LPNs and RNs functioned side by side every day, doing the same work except for the above mentioned items. What struck me then was that many of the LPNs I worked with were actually better nurses than some of the RNs, but would never make as much money or be given administrative positions. The initials count.

Of course, the lowest rung on the nursing staff is occupied by the nursing assistants or nurses' aides. Even within that job description, there is a hierarchy. At the top, are the so-called "med-aides." These nursing assistants have had advanced training and are allowed to pass medications in nursing homes. Regular nursing assistants could not touch medications in the hospital. Next in line were the Certified Nursing Assistants (CNA). That's what I was. The certification signified that we had taken a course in nursing assisting at a hospital, or, in my case, at the community college. Below us were the old fashioned, on-the-job trained nurses' aides. These folks were being phased out of the hospital where I worked by attrition - you couldn't be hired in 1977 unless you had passed the certification course.

* * *

This hierarchy was probably the cause for much of the personnel problems in the hospital. These dedicated health providers were viewed administratively as a set of initials rather than as individuals who had varying talents and gifts. I can tell you for certain that the patient had very little interest in the initials on the caregiver's name tag.

Jean was a cancer patient who was admitted to my floor around Thanksgiving. That summer, she had been apparently healthy, playing softball and enjoying her two small children. By the time I met Jean, she weighed eighty pounds and was in the end stages of cancer which had metastasized from her spine. She had lost all of her hair and was in a great deal of pain. For some reason, Jean took a liking to me, and, until she died on Valentine's Day the next year, wouldn't let anyone except me help her into a chair or onto the commode if she knew I was in the hospital.

I will never forget the night that she had slipped down into her bed from having the head raised. The head nurse on that shift wanted to help boost her up in bed. Jean had the nurse page me, and the "boss" and I went into her room together. "She wants me to move up in bed, Kent," Jean said with a concerned look on her face. It hurt her to even think about being moved. She continued, "What do you think?" Jean didn't know (or care, for that matter) that she was asking a lowly CNA for his opinion on the head nurse's recommendation.  I thought it was a good idea, and up in bed Jean went.

Of course, I'll never forget Jean for many reasons, but one of the lessons I learned from her is that initials behind a person's name, position on the ladder of professional success, and salaries and titles are not the bottom line in health care.  Patients have always known this, but we the health professionals are taking longer to figure it out.

* * *

The pecking order which I have described in the nursing profession is based somewhat on education.  As with any health profession, additional education should drive legislative efforts to increase the profession's scope of practice.  The lines become blurred, however, when the two year diploma nurse and the BSN both have the same license.  Even less recognizable is the generic title "nurse" which can mean anything from a one year LPN to a master's prepared nurse practitioner.

In some ways, this dichotomy within the nursing profession is reminiscent of the dichotomy of practice styles which exists in the chiropractic profession.  As we have seen, these differences have resulted from geographic location, the educational era of the chiropractor, and which school the chiropractor attended.  In the same way that nurses bemoan the fact that the public has no good way to tell them apart, the chiropractic profession also suffers from the lack of distinction.

The hierarchy model which I have described places chiropractors on the third tier. Chiropractic has traditionally been described as an "alternative" health profession, one which is outside the medical model. Chiropractors aren't sure that the "alternative" adjective still applies to their profession.

There has been an effort to "mainstream" chiropractic which has been reasonably successful. Mainstream chiropractic views itself as a primary care service which emphasizes a team approach to health.

Even so, doctors of chiropractic are highly autonomous practitioners. Licensing of chiropractors within the United States began in 1910 in Kansas, and was completed by 1973 when Louisiana became the last state to license DCs. In addition, the state licensing boards are controlled by chiropractors in forty-seven states. In the remaining three states, licensing is overseen by a "mixed" board consisting of medical doctors, osteopaths, chiropractors, and other health professionals.

Self-regulation is an important characteristic of any profession. The chiropractic profession is essentially self-regulating and, therefore, quite autonomous. The fact that traditional medicine does not regulate or oversee chiropractic has caused numerous professional clashes in the past. The competition between the professions was intense for years. Neither side would yield to the other on any issue. Economics and arrogance on the part of the medical doctors, and a defensive, minority status stubbornness on the part of chiropractors kept the two groups apart.

This hierarchical system, then, has produced several results over the years. From the patient's perspective, the hierarchy produces confusion and distrust, and ultimately denies the patient freedom of provider choice and appropriate referral. Patients are harmed financially by insurance company prejudice against certain providers. Patients have suffered untold months and years of poor health because of the stubborn reluctance of providers to refer patients to non-traditional practitioners.

* * *

Mary was a professional fifty year old woman who had suffered headaches for years. She recounted that she had been through every diagnostic test known to man to try to figure out the cause of the headaches.

"All of the tests came up negative, doc," she recounted, "but the headaches continued. Finally, my doctors gave up on me and referred me to a psychiatrist who prescribed anti-depressant medications. I don't have clinical depression; rather, I was depressed because I was unable to function with the headaches! I didn't take that medication, but I was increasingly relying on pain medication just to get through the day. My life was no longer my own."

"One day I mentioned the headaches to my dentist. He told me the headaches were related to my bite, and began to treat me for TMJ dysfunction. Hundreds of dollars and months later with no results, he told me that I would just have to live with the problem."

"I had never been to a chiropractor before, and I never thought that a chiropractor could help me with something in my head. Finally, a friend of mine at work recommended that I see you."

This story is very typical of what a chiropractor often hears in his office. Fortunately, Mary had headaches which were vertebrogenic in origin (caused by dysfunction in her neck) and responded to chiropractic treatment. If she had just been referred to a chiropractor by the medical doctor or dentist, she could have been evaluated and treated much earlier.

* * *

How has the medical system hierarchy affected the practitioners from the third tier? When a person's profession is devalued and disrespected by the larger medical system, how does the minority profession respond? Why do patients use the services of "nontraditional" providers despite the lack of encouragement and even slander from the traditional medical system? How do these professions survive?

* * *

I clearly remember my first experience with discrimination against chiropractic. When I was a junior high school student, I injured my back in gym class. Because he had had a positive experience with a chiropractor earlier in his life, my dad decided that mine was a chiropractic problem. Dad took me to the chiropractor in our town, a gentle elderly man. After listening to me tell him about my problem, Doc Christiansen began to treat me. He also wrote me an excuse for physical education class for the week.

When I presented the excuse to my gym teacher, a man whom I liked and respected, he took one look at it and sneered, "Chiropractors aren't *real* doctors, Kent. They can't write prescriptions."

I was crushed and embarrassed by his scornful remark. My parents had decided that the chiropractor was the doctor I needed for my problem; but in a few words, the coach had discounted their decision with his "superior" knowledge. I am still enraged that a fully licensed health professional who had probably been serving patients for thirty or forty years could be so easily dismissed by an ignorant physical education teacher. I didn't tell my parents, of course, but I felt differently about Doc Christiansen from that time on.

* * *

One of the tasks I enjoyed doing as a hospital nursing assistant was to man the "call board" at the nursing station when the unit secretary took her coffee break.  I was answering calls one day when the patient in room 620 called and asked for his pain medication.  I looked at the cardex to see the patient's name, and was surprised to see that he was a doctor.  (Doctors usually get special treatment  when they are patients in the hospital.)

"Dr. McCarthy is calling for his pain meds," I called to the nurse who was in charge of his hall that day.

"I didn't know there was a doctor on the floor," one of the aides piped in.

The nurse walked to her medication cart and sighed.  "He's a *chiropractor*," she said disdainfully, as if she couldn't stand to have the term "doctor" used so loosely.

* * *

My friend Dave, an LPN, mentioned  to his wife's gynecologist that he was a chiropractic student.

"What a waste of a career," was the unsolicited reply.

How many patients had the gynecologist dissuaded from seeing a chiropractor with similar comments?

* * *

Early chiropractors reacted to the medical devaluation of their profession in several ways. Many of them quietly continued to practice their profession despite the prevalent perception of the medical profession.  Others became quite vocal and argumentative in return, deepening the chasm between the profession and causing even more confusion among patients. The chiropractic zealots overstated the potential of the profession by claiming that they could successfully treat any health problem with chiropractic adjustments. The medical profession countered with warnings that this idea was ridiculous. On and on it went.

Surprisingly, the chiropractic profession did not buckle in the midst of this undesirable atmosphere and agree to become subservient to the MD. It seems that the more tenacious the MDs were, the more the chiropractic profession grew. Patients continued to visit chiropractors (presumably) because of the health results they obtained.

In the post-Watergate years, people from all walks of life began to question all kinds of traditional authority. The political medical authority, the AMA, was no exception. Both patients and other health professionals first questioned and then began to challenge the medical profession through appropriate and pro-active channels - legislative action, lawsuits, and increased communication and public relations on issues which are at the heart of the hierarchy. The pecking order was beginning to be challenged.

In addition, patients began to be disappointed and disillusioned by medicine's excesses. Many patients began to question if drugs and surgery were the only way to keep healthy. A wellness movement was beginning in the US with patients investigating nutrition, exercise, preventative medicine and other lifestyle issues on their own. Former traditional patients began to discover chiropractic, acupuncture, biofeedback and other conservative health management methods. Chiropractic health care was inviting to patients because of its conservative, preventative approach to the patient.

The health care landscape was beginning to change. Other practitioners began to say to medicine, "We have a service to provide which is equal to or better than the service you provide." Optometrists lobbied for the right to treat eye disease. Chiropractors began to fight the medical establishment for the right to practice in hospitals. Psychologists and podiatrists began to be included in insurance coverage.

These providers pointed out the strengths in their professional education and practice. Chiropractors showed their expertise and training in the neuromusculoskeletal system, in clinical nutrition and in manual treatment, all far superior to medical school. Other professions did the same. With the facts out, the idea that medical doctors should be consulted to see if chiropractors are any good at what they do seems ridiculous. Medical doctors, by virtue of their education, do not possess the skills or tools necessary to evaluate chiropractic practice.

* * *

One of the interesting parallels one can draw from this brief examination of the nursing profession regards the medical doctor's apparent approval of expanded roles for nurses. MDs have welcomed the increase in professionalization in nursing as long as the nurse is still connected to them by the umbilical cord of the collegial relationship. Medical practitioners have hired nurse practitioners and physician assistants (who, by law, have the same sort of relationship) to screen patients, do physical exams, treat common illnesses, and make housecalls. The hierarchy is maintained.

Medical doctor's relationships with the third tier in my model is not so self-serving. Recognizing other practitioners, like chiropractic doctors who do not require the MDs prescription, does not directly benefit the medical doctor in any way. In fact, such recognition that other health providers have important contributions to make in a patient's health is seen as weakening the medical doctor's grip on the pinnacle of this traditional hierarchy.

Because this recognition does benefit the patient, however, a few liberal medical doctors have taken the position recently that the professions should better work together. This revelation, while some one hundred years late, should be welcomed by the health care consumer, who will benefit ultimately from the improved relations.

# 8

# <u>Reformation</u>

Health care system reform is imminent in the United States. With thirty-eight million people unable to afford health insurance at all, and an untold number of others who have inadequate access to the health care they require, the situation has become a major crisis in our country.

Discussion about the health care system is taking place daily. Business and industry, politicians, social scientists, public policy analysts, and health care providers are all looking for solutions. These discussions bring new phrases to describe the solution to this widespread problem. Phrases like managed health care, basic packages of medical care, and appropriation of health care dollars are being thrown about. Many health care providers are worried that they will not make the public policy cut. The services that they provide and their very livelihoods hang in the balance of these discussions.

Perhaps in this time of whirlwind spotlighting and change in the health system, it is also time to re-evaluate and end the discrimination, prejudice, and distrust which exists between licensed health care providers. With the hierarchical system unable to adequately address the health care needs of the country's citizens, it is possible that a "new order" would do a better job.

* * *

How can a "new order" come about when there is so much ignorance on the part of providers about other providers?  How would a medical doctor know when it was appropriate  to refer to a chiropractor?   How would a chiropractor  know what a nurse practitioner  could do for a patient?  How can the osteopath  be assured  that the medical doctor he refers to won't try to coerce the patient into seeking a new health  manager?   And, as a patient, how can I be sure that the manager I have chosen will refer me when necessary?  How can I be sure that my health  manager  doesn't have prejudice against all other  types of primary  care providers?

The plan which I envision  for the  coming  decades  includes  four fundamental  changes in the roles of health  care  providers.   All of these changes are designed  toward the goal of a more harmonious  and eventually, a more effective health  care  system.   The four arms of this public policy change include: professional definition of strengths and limitations, built into revised licensing laws if necessary;  required  education  about  other  health professions  as a prerequisite  to licensing;   federally  funded,  independent clinical research to investigate professional claims of efficacy and to encourage interdependence  of the health  professions;  and the introduction  of a health manager  system on a pilot study basis. These changes will take some time to complete.   However,  if the change  is going  to be part  of a permanent restructuring  effort,  the time will be well spent.   This is not a band-aid solution, but directed  toward  a more  equitable  and viable relationship between  providers.

## Professional  Definition

A profession's scope of practice law should be consistent with the practitioners' education.  Recognition of professional limits should come from within the profession itself, not from a self-designated "gatekeeper" who is essentially uninformed about other professions.  Self regulation is one of the hallmarks of a profession which must be preserved.

The chiropractic scopes of practice are highly variable from state to state.  Many of the licensing laws were written years ago, when the education of a chiropractor was quite different from what it is today.  Some states restrict chiropractic doctors from providing services in which they are fully trained.  These restrictions effectively prevent doctors of chiropractic from functioning as primary care physicians, which is how they are educated in school.

Indiana and Massachusetts laws expressly forbid chiropractors from treating "or attempting to treat" infectious diseases.  Taken to the limit, these statutes would prevent the chiropractor from managing even a viral infection or the common cold.  New York's law goes one step further, to name systems and disorders which it considers outside the chiropractor's scope of practice. DCs in New York "...maynot treat any of the cardio-vascular-renal or cardio-pulmonary diseases, ...or diabetes..." New Jersey places limitations on the common chiropractic service of nutritional counseling:  "...the chiropractic physician ...shall not represent himself or herself as a nutritional consultant and shall not sell or dispense vitamins, food products or nutritional supplements."  New Jersey's law for medical doctors contains no such stipulation, even though chiropractors have much more education in nutrition than MDs.  Pennsylvania grants DCs the right to diagnose patients, "... provided that such diagnosis is necessary to determine the nature and appropriateness of chiropractic treatment."  (Chiropractic (or any health system) treatment *without* diagnosis would indeed be dangerous for the patient!)    Virginia's law may currently contain the most restrictive of the definitions of chiropractic:  "Practice of chiropractic means the adjustment of the twenty-four moveable vertebrae of the spinal column."

Currently, Illinois and Vermont have the broadest scope of practice for chiropractors.   Illinois' definition of the practice of chiropractic reads, "The treatment of human ailments without the use of drugs and without operative surgery."  The Vermont definition states that "the practice of chiropractic consists of diagnosing and treating human ailments without the use of prescription drugs or surgery." These definitions are obviously quite different from Virginia's above.   Other states, like Arizona, allow for a primary care role, but emphasize the musculoskeletal system with regard to treatment:

> A Doctor of Chiropractic is a portal of entry health care provider who engages in the practice of health care which includes:
> 1. The practice of health care which deals with the diagnosis and correction of subluxations, functional vertebral or articular dysarthrosis or neuromuscular skeletal disorders for the restoration and maintenance of health.
> 2. The use of physical and clinical examination, diagnostic x-rays and clinical laboratory procedures by referral in order to determine the propriety of a regimen of chiropractic care or to form a basis for referral of patients to other licensed health care professionals, or both.
> 3. Treatment by adjustment of the spine or bodily articulations and those procedures preparatory and complementary to such adjustments, including physiotherapy and traction related to the correction of subluxations or orthopedic supports of the spine and acupuncture by certification.

In addition to recognizing professional limits, the problem of diverse competencies in providers who have been trained in years past must be addressed.   Since a chiropractor trained as recently as 1970 did not, at some schools, study physical diagnosis, laboratory diagnosis, or other subjects necessary to be a primary health care provider, how can the chiropractic license accurately reflect these practitioners' training?

Currently, seventeen states have separate, additional certifications for certain procedures. The chiropractic license is the same for all DCs, but if that DC wants to use acupuncture or physiotherapy procedures, for example, the applicant must demonstrate education in that subject and take an additional exam. Only then will he or she be allowed to practice these procedures. Florida, for instance, has four certifications in addition to the generic chiropractic license: physiotherapy, phlebotomy (venipuncture for blood sample collection), acupuncture, and proprietary drugs ("prescribing" or recommending over-the-counter medications). Oklahoma has certification in acupuncture and injectable vitamins and minerals.

The certification process accomplishes two purposes. First, it allows the chiropractor to provide services for which he/she is trained and competent. Second, this is accomplished without sacrificing public interest by making sure that providers who have not been trained in these procedures cannot perform them.

In a generation, most practicing chiropractors will have been trained in accredited schools with homogenous curricula. The problem of varying competencies will be somewhat eliminated. Additional certifications, then, could be expunged from the state practice laws.

As I have explained, chiropractors are still not completely united as to their role in health care. Some feel strongly that chiropractors should function as primary health care providers, while others wish to be considered spinal specialists. Nevertheless, chiropractic colleges are, and have been for a number of years, training their students as portal of entry health care providers. The best thinking on the dichotomy of practice styles appears to be to make the practice laws as broad as possible as long as they do not infringe on those who want to practice more narrowly, and as long as the public interest is protected.

The next step in the self-definition of a profession is in the development of a unified standard of practice. Chiropractors have, thus far, been very slow to come up with profession-wide standards. In 1990, leaders in the profession met to address this shortcoming. The profession recognized that a nation-wide standards of care for the chiropractic patient was essential in order to continue growing as a mainstream health profession. Over the next two years, leaders met to develop a consensus on various treatment issues. In 1992, a 225 page document was produced and distributed to every chiropractor in the US. Called the Mercy Center Conference Guidelines, this document addresses issues of diagnosis methods, appropriateness of care, and frequency, duration, and type of care for a variety of commonly treated conditions. It should be extremely helpful to chiropractic educators, practicing chiropractors, third party payers, attorneys, and other health professions in helping to more clearly define what it is that chiropractors do.


## Education


Once a profession has some sort of consensus on their own professional activities, interdisciplinary education can begin to take place. The second arm of the health system reformation must include education for all providers on the various health professions. These courses should be required in the undergraduate professional curriculum as well as in a post-graduate format as a requirement for licensing. The purpose of the course is to increase understanding about various professional activities and training, as well as to begin to break down prejudices among health providers.

One of the most important aspects of the course should be a detailed description of each profession's educational process. Much of the prejudice against chiropractors by other providers is due to ignorance. Coursework, quality of faculty, accreditation, research efforts, student profiles, physical plant, and clinical aspects of the educational process should be emphasized. The history of the development of the profession would be useful in dispelling archaic rumors which have a tendency to stick to a profession.

Following the description of the educational process, a description of the practice methods of each type of provider should be presented. Diagnostic and therapeutic skills that are common to the professions should be related. Any diagnostic skills unique to a profession and their efficacy should be described and demonstrated. Treatment methods which are both similar and dissimilar should be described and demonstrated. In this way, providers will better understand to whom a patient should be referred and the procedures which that provider is likely to recommend.

Health care providers of all kinds should be encouraged to recognize the sociological aspects of the hierarchy as it currently exists. All types of health providers should be encouraged to recognize interdependence which would benefit their patients. Recognizing interdependencies is the first step toward the ultimate goal of a team approach to health care.

Heavy emphasis should be placed on scientific studies showing efficacy of treatment. The natural suspicion which exists between professions can only be dispelled with research. Chiropractors would benefit from understanding surgical procedures and pharmacological treatment, surgeons should be interested in alternative treatments for patients who do not require surgery, obstetricians could be enlightened as to why pregnant women prefer midwives for delivery.

Can all the prejudices of decades past be dispelled with this type of education?  Of course not.  However, the goal is to create a new generation of health care providers who are willing to put the patient's benefit first by being open minded enough to allow for freedom of choice.  Further, health providers must realize that there is not enough money to pay for health care in this country.  Procedures which are found to be cost-effective, regardless of the practitioner who provides the service, must be enveloped by the system.


## Research


What services does a fair and equitable basic health package include? This is an important question facing our country.  Beyond this basic package, persons who can afford to add services would be welcome to do so.  The basic package of health care should strive for equity among all currently licensed and recognized health professions.  These professions have shown by simple supply and demand economics that they are beneficial.  The interesting phenomenon of the growth of the chiropractic profession despite bitter opposition is testament to this fact.  Patients will not continue to return to a health professional from whom they obtain no health benefits.

This basic package should include treatment for common and uncommon illnesses which plague the citizens of our country.  The idea is that a package would be created which would guarantee the citizen that the best and most cost effective treatment will be available for them, no matter what health crisis they are facing.

The basic package must address the care of musculoskeletal problems, which account for some eighty-five million episodes of ill health every year in this country. It must guarantee care for mental health, treatment of chemical dependency and treatment of national epidemics like AIDS. In addition, it must provide for a patient's freedom of choice of providers among all currently licensed health professionals.    Research funding must be provided to all groups of practitioners in order to ascertain what types of treatments are most efficacious, reliable, and cost effective for various health problems. Study designs which emphasize co-management and interdependence of various professions could provide new and exciting alliances in the world of health care. At present, no provider group except the medical doctors can afford to carry out this research in isolation. Federal health research funding is not dispersed equitably between various health professions. This problem of discrimination must be ended in order to design a useful and equitable policy.


## The Health Manager


The development of a true team approach to health care would benefit the patient in many ways. Patients would be made aware of their choice of a primary health care provider who could be designated as their "health manager." At the present time, providers trained, licensed, and recognized as primary care providers include medical doctors with certain specialties like family practice, internal medicine, and pediatrics; osteopathic doctors with similar specialties, certain nurse practitioners, and chiropractors. These health care professionals have been trained to evaluate the entire human body, and then treat or refer to the appropriate specialist. They are "portals of entry" into the health care system.

Patients should be assured that whomever they choose for a health care manager enjoys appropriate professional relationships with other providers.

Diagnostic tests should not have to be repeated by a specialist; the two providers should be willing to work together to co-manage the patient in appropriate situations, there should be mutual trust between the providers, and the patient should not be subject to coercion to abandon his/her original choice of manager.

Patients would develop enough trust in their manager that he/she could recommend visits to other providers in certain situations, rather than the patient trying to make his/her way through the complicated maze of health care alone (the current system.) Health care dollars could be saved by eliminating inappropriate or unfruitful doctor visits, initiated by patients who can't successfully navigate the system alone. The patient would be more likely to spend his/her health care dollars wisely, and receive better health care, too.

The health manager system requires providers to pay attention to health care costs. Medical waste and fraud consumes millions of dollars annually from our health care budget.

* * *

Is this plan for restructuring the roles of health care providers' relationships a dream? Yes.

Is it impossible to imagine? Not at all.

All over the United States, interdiscipinary health care clinics are springing up where providers of all kinds work together. Even if these clinics are originally set up merely for convenience or economic advantage, the interaction between the providers is healthy and desirable. Encouragement should be forthcoming to increase the numbers of these types of clinics.

Books such as this one are contributions to the understanding of various health professions. I have read many like it authored by midwives, surgeons, psychologists, and podiatrists. Books of this kind have increased my understanding of their professions, and my respect for these practitioners.

Classes are being taught to future health professionals about health care roles and contributions. I am lucky to teach such a course to future chiropractors. In this course, I attempt to enlighten students about the education, training and professional contributions of chiropractic and other health professions. One of the goals of such a course is to encourage new chiropractic graduates to network with other health professionals for the benefit of their patients. I see similar courses being taught at some other types of professional schools.

Interdisciplinary research is being done, albeit on an extremely small scale. Professionals in the research field must continue to write grant proposals which would encourage such studies. Funding for such research is vital in light of the current crisis.

The health manager plan that includes professions in addition to medical doctors and osteopathic doctors is a dream. Although federal designations and (most) state licensing laws recognize chiropractors and nurse practitioners as primary care providers, the "good old boy" system of hierarchy still exists. Working within the system, change can occur, but it extremely slow and frustrating work.

* * *

Recently, my professional ethics class discussed the topic of interdisciplinary relations. After a spirited debate about the ethics of referral and patient freedom of choice, a hand went up in the lecture hall.

"Dr. Boyer," the student began, "do you mean that, ideally, all health professionals could eventually be represented by just one professional organization whose ultimate goal would be superior health care for the patient? We could end all of the fighting among health providers because it is counter-productive? That health providers would respect one another enough to work together? Isn't that a little idealistic?"

A great question. Positive changes occur ultimately as a result of idealism, sometimes blind idealism. The future generation of health care providers must provide such idealism, and I think that they will.